DATE			

VICTOR HUGO

HENRI PEYRE

VICTOR
HUGO

PHILOSOPHY AND POETRY

translated by
RODA P. ROBERTS

The University of Alabama Press
University, Alabama

Library of Congress Cataloging in Publication Data
Peyre, Henri, 1901–
    Victor Hugo, philosophy and poetry.
    Translation of Hugo.
    Bibliography: p.
    Includes index.
    1. Hugo, Victor Marie, comte, 1802–1885.
2. Authors, French—19th century—Biography.
PQ2293.P313   848'.7'09 [B]   79-9876
ISBN 0-8173-0017-1

Translated into English from
Hugo, sa vie, son oeuvre
Copyright © 1972 by
Presses Universitaires de France

CONTENTS

TRANSLATOR'S PREFACE

Much ink has been spilled on Hugo the man and Hugo the writer. The selective bibliography at the end of Henri Peyre's work is a clear indication of this fact. And yet, there always seems something left unsaid of the multiple facets of this great romanticist. Thus, M. Peyre, while returning to an old and familiar subject, has been able in his work to add a new perspective. A great merit of his book, in my opinion, is that he has struck a happy balance between the extremes found in many of the writings on Hugo. Instead of blindly hailing Hugo as the greatest writer of verse since time immemorial, Peyre has presented him as a man who had something to say and who knew how to say it well; instead of loudly proclaiming him as the greatest philosopher of nineteenth-century France, Peyre has analyzed with great sensitivity Hugo's thoughts on a wide variety of subjects. And unlike some of the authors of books and articles on Hugo's philosophy, Peyre has not hesitated to admit that certain elements of it remain vague and even to bring out apparent contradictions. But while stressing the unsystematic nature of Hugo's ideas, Peyre has managed nevertheless to put together a global picture of the romanticist's philosophy and to convince even the most skeptical reader that Hugo *was* a thinker, if not a philosopher in the true sense of the term.

What adds great value to this work, as opposed to others on Hugo's philosophy, is the large number of quotations from Hugo's works that have been skilfully intertwined into Peyre's text, and the extracts—many of them little known to most—added at the end of the book to illustrate particular aspects of Hugo's thinking. But what makes Peyre's work particularly interesting also makes it very difficult to translate. And had it not been for the many quotations and extracts, I would not have felt the need to add a translator's preface. But having been faced with the difficult task of translating not only Peyre but also Hugo, I felt it incumbent on me to bring out some pertinent points.

When the question of translating *Hugo* was first broached, there was an important decision to be made. Should the quotations from Hugo be left in French or not? There seemed, however, little point in translating the work if the quotations from Hugo were left in the original language, for surely if readers could understand Hugo in French they could understand Peyre in French. Therefore, the decision was taken to render everything in English, including Hugo's verse and prose.

The next stage was to try and find as many of Hugo's works already available in translation as possible. This was a frustrating period, for a tour of four major libraries revealed that, while most of Hugo's novels and plays had already been translated, few of his poems had been, and most of these were "anthology pieces" that Peyre had not quoted. There was no option, therefore, but to translate most of the quotations and longer extracts from Hugo's works.

The translation of the prose extracts not available in English was not all that difficult. It involved the usual problems of literary translation. First, the appropriate level of language had to be maintained, e.g., "Si la mort est pour l'homme la fin de tout, peu importe ce qu'il a fait durant la vie." / "If death is the end of everything for man, then what he has done in life is of little importance." (*Le tas de pierres* / *Pile of Stones*) Given the elevated level of language used by Hugo in this extract, rendering "peu importe" as "does not really matter" would not have been justified. It should be noted that the level of language in all the prose extracts, even those taken from Adèle Hugo's diary, is relatively formal.

Second, the various stylistic features that abound in Hugo's work must be suitably dealt with. Such features have presumably been employed by Hugo, as they are by authors in general, for the sake of impact and aesthetic appeal. Thus, rather than merely aping in translation a given stylistic feature of the French text, I have endeavored to analyze its effect and then decide if the same feature, when it does exist in English, is functionally equivalent; when this is not the case, or when the same formal feature is little used in English, I have tried to find a different but functionally equivalent feature to match the French, and in some cases I have resorted to "compensating" for the loss of a specialized feature elsewhere in the text.

Listed below are a few of the stylistic features encountered, along with their translation and with comments.

1. Repetition: e.g. 1: *Journal de l'exil / The Diary of Exile,* Paragraph 1:

In this paragraph, the repetition, which is mainly lexical, seems to have been used to bring out the argumentation as clearly and strongly as possible. It has been retained to a large extent in English.

e.g. 2: *Le tas de pierres / Pile of Stones,* Paragraph 1:

"L'homme juste et le méchant sont traités de la *même* manière par la *même* fin." / "The righteous and the wicked are treated in the *same* manner by death, which awaits them all."

In this case, the repetition of "même" has not been retained in the English, as "fin" was rendered by "death" and "the same death" would have been meaningless. However, I have tried to reproduce the effect of insistence and solemnity created by the repetition in French by the subordinate clause "which awaits them all" (attempt at "immediate compensation").

2. Anaphora: This rhetorical device of repeating a word or phrase at the beginning of successive clauses or sentences is found in several of the prose extracts. As in the case of repetition in general, the effect created is one of force. Anaphora has normally been retained in the English translation.

e.g. 1: *Journal de l'exil / The Diary of Exile,* Second extract, Paragraph 1:

"*Laissez* cette branche d'arbre; *laissez* cette feuille,..." / "*Leave* the branch alone; *leave* the leaf alone."

e.g. 2: *Paroles rapportées par Stapfer* / *Remarks Recorded by Stapfer:*

"*Il est* l'Auteur de tout. *Il est* le Créateur. (. . .) *Il est* l'âme de l'univers. *Il est* le Moi de l'infini.*" / "He is* the Maker of everything. *He is* the Creator. (. . .) *He is* the soul of the universe. *He is* the Self of the infinite."

3. *Anacoluthon:* A change from one grammatical construction to another within the same sentence is sometimes used as a rhetorical device. There was one striking example in Hugo's prose extracts. I decided, however, to avoid it in translation, as a shift in construction most often denotes poor writing and I felt that such a shift would have contributed nothing from the point of view of effect in translation.

e.g.: *Promontorium Somnii,* Second extract, Paragraph 7:

"Quelle extravagance que la fougère de cinq cents pieds de haut! les houillères la constatent." / "It seems absurd to imagine ferns five hundred feet tall, and yet coal-pits bear witness to this."

4. *Figures of speech:* Hugo's prose, as much as his poetry, abounds in figures of speech. I have tried to retain as many of them as possible, although in some cases I have replaced one figure by another which fitted better into the translation.

e.g. 1: *Promontorium Somnii,* Second extract, Paragraph 5:

"Aujourd'hui, dans l'Occident, on livre son âme au tabac, ce sombre *endormeur* de la civilisation d'Europe." / "Today, the West is seeking oblivion in tobacco, that somber *sandman* of European civilization." (Metaphor/Metaphor)

e.g. 2: *Le tas de pierres / Pile of Stones:*
Car quel plus grand mal que l'absence du bien?
Cela n'est-il pas evident? *L'absence du jour, c'est la nuit: l'absence du bien, c'est le mal...*

For what evil could be greater than the lack of good?
Is this not obvious? *Just as when it is not day it is night,*
So also when there is no good there is evil . . .
(Implicit comparison / Simile)

5. *Rhetorical question:*   This device, which, according to
Hilaire Belloc, is more common in French than in English, has
been frequently used by Hugo, and it has generally been retained
in translation as it helps to reinforce basic philosophical points,
which if presented as statements would sound trite.

e.g.: *Promontorium Somnii*
"La nature jadis n'a-t-elle pas rêvé aussi? Le monde ne s'est-il
pas ébauché par un songe? N'y a-t-il pas du nuage dans le
premier effort de la création?" / Has nature not dreamed its
dreams at one time? Was the world not shaped by a dream?
Did reverie not figure in the first attempt at creation?"

These are just a few of the many stylistic features found in
Hugo's prose extracts. And all these devices are equally found in
Hugo's poetry. For, in fact, the prose of this great romanticist
often resembles poetry. And the only reason I have chosen to
discuss separately the translation of Hugo's prose and that of his
poems is that the latter involved choices in the area of prosody
that were obviously not required for the former.

The translation of poetry has always been a very controversial
topic. The American poet Robert Frost coined the classic phrase:
"Poetry is what gets lost in translation." This was initially the
fear of Henri Peyre when the question of translating Hugo first
arose. I, as a translator, was aware of the fact that the translation
of Hugo's poems would prove a very difficult task, but was willing
on reflection to accept the challenge.

One of the first points to be resolved was to decide whether or
not to abide by the cardinal principle of Professor Postgate (expressed in *Translation and Translations*) whereby verse should be

translated by verse—an opinion upheld in varying degrees by men such as Carlyle, Leigh Hunt, and Lord Woodhouselee. But is "verse" a synonym of poetry? To be sure, much poetry is in verse form, i.e., it is composed of a metrical arrangement of words (and often includes rhyme and stanza form), but poetry lies partially outside the area of verse in that some poetry is not written in metrical language (e.g., the so-called "free verse"), while there is an area of verse (represented for example by the lines: "Thirty days has September, // April, June and November") that remains outside the area of poetry. Hence, Professor Postgate's principle was poorly founded to begin with. The question that should therefore be posed is "What makes poetry?". An answer that, although vague, puts us on the right track has been provided by Ewald Osers in "Some Aspects of the Translation of Poetry," *Meta*, 23:1 (March 1978):

> If we accept that a formal metre-and-rhyme framework is no longer the criterion of poetry, and if—as I hope—we also accept that prose chopped up into short lines does not make poetry, we must clearly look for its specific characteristics in the linguistic texture. I believe that the true criterion of poetry—one that is equally applicable to metre-and-rhyme verse and to unrhymed poetry—is the internal tension, or temperature, or charge of the language. [. . .] A word, a group of words, or a phrase derives its tension, its charge, its impact on the reader or listener from its 'otherness', from the way it differs from ordinary speech, from the novelty of its employment in a particular context, from the surprise it produces. All these concepts—otherness, difference, novelty, surprise—presuppose comparison. Comparison with a norm, with customary usage. It follows therefore, that no word or turn of phrase can carry that extra charge that makes it poetry unless there is an alternative, unless the poetic text represents a deliberate choice from among possible options. The question: Is there an alternative? is therefore, in my opinion, central to the whole problem of poetry, and of translating poetry. It is the deliberate choice from among available alternatives that gives a word, or a line, its emotional temperature or charge.

Considered from this point of view, the translation of poetry, while being far from easy, does become possible for someone who is not a versewriter but who has a feel for poetic language, someone like me for instance.

I thus began by making two deliberate general choices regarding rhyme and meter. Hugo's poems, even the most philosophical, are in rhyme. Since rhyme imposes a constraint upon a translator, a constraint which bears most heavily on the essential feature of the translation of poetry, the choice of words to retain an emotional charge, and since the introduction of rhyme often leads the translator to take some liberty with the ideas of the original, I felt that it would be best to avoid seeking at all cost rhyme in the strict sense of the word (i.e., end rhyme or the repetition of identical or closely similar sounds at the end of verses).

Where, almost unbeknownst to me, a kind of imperfect end rhyme crept in because of the lexical choice made for other reasons, I of course welcomed the musicality thus created:

e.g.: *La science et l'absolu / Science and the Absolute:*
Si tu n'étais science, on te croirait envie.
De la nature pourpre auguste de la vie,
Vous faites un haillon, ô vivants, un lambeau,
Une loque, un néant; et le ver du tombeau
Nomme cela manger; vous l'appelez connaître.
Toi savoir! tu ne peux que décomposer l'être!

If your name were not science, it could well have been envy.
You, the living, reduce the august cloak of life—nature—
To rags and tatters, to nothingness;
And while the worms in graves call that *eating,*
You call that *learning.*
Oh knowledge! All you can do is decompose the *being!*

However, even such imperfect end rhyme is almost nonexistent in my translations. But, while rhyme in the strict sense of the word is absent, I have tried to include, as much as possible, rhyme in the more general sense of any repetition of the same or closely similar sounds to create a musical effect and an emotional charge. Thus, alliteration, assonance, and consonance are frequently found in my translations of Hugo.

Alliteration:

e.g. 1: *La science et l'absolu / Science and the Absolute*
C'est en dêchiquetant que vous croyez trouver.
You *th*ink you can find the answers by tearing *th*ings apart.

e.g. 2: *Ah! La philosophie est vorace / Oh! Philosophy is Insatiable*
Regarde. On est en route. On fuit le long des grèves.
Toute la Grèce rit comme un palais de rêves.
L'ardent vaisseau qui traîne à travers le flot bleu
Ses noirs poumons de houille et son souffle de feu
Voit défiler les caps, les îlots, les calanques.

Look! the journey has begun. The *sh*ip glides along the *sh*ore.
All Greece seems like a world of dreams.
The *thr*obbing vessel, which makes its way *thr*ough the *bl*ue waters
Its lungs *bl*ack with coal and its breath *f*ull of *f*ire,
Drifts past headlands, islets and inlets.

Assonance:

e.g.: *La science et l'absolu / Science and the Absolute*
Il ne sait pas si c'est cinq minutes qu'il faut
A la lumière, au fond des obscurités bleues,
Pour franchir trente-cinq millions de vos lieues,
Et venir du soleil, braise de l'infini,
A la terre, affreux globe, impur, lépreux, banni,
Roulant dans votre amas d'ombres inférieures, . . .

It does not know if light takes five minutes
To travel thirty-five million leagues through the blue depths

From the sun, the fire of the infinite,
To the earth, that frightful globe, impure, diseased and
exiled,
Rolling around in the host of shadows down below; . . .

Consonance:

e.g.: *Dieu / God*
. . . Dante envahit la nuit cercle par cercle;
Spinoza du néant lève l'affreux couvercle;
Fulton dompte la mer que Xercès révolta;
Galvani forge et mêle, à côté de Volta,
Les fluides, force, âme, aimants, métaux, mercures;
Mesmer tressaillant touche aux frontières obscures; . . .

Dante penetrated the dark depths, circle by circle;
Spinoza revealed the dreadful secrets of nothingness;
Fulton tamed the sea stirred up by Xerxes;
Galvani, followed by Volta, handled and mixed
Fluids, power, core, magnets, metals and mercury;
Mesmer, filled with awe, discovered unknown horizons.

Sometimes the choice of words led not just to alliteration,
assonance, or consonance but to internal rhyme.

Internal rhyme:

e.g.: *La science et l'absolu / Science and the Absolute*
La foudre dont tremblaient le mage et le druide,
O savants, à cette heure est pour vous un fluide
Forcé d'être vitreux s'il n'est pas résineux; . . .

The thunderbolt that caused the magus and the druid to
tremble
Now is for you scientists only a fluid
Which has to be vitreous if it is not resinous.

Thus, in the translation of all the poetic extracts of Hugo, I
have endeavored to maintain the musicality of sounds, although

I have not attempted a strict rhyme pattern at the end of each verse.

When dealing with the rhythm of Hugo's poems, I have borne in mind that meter "has no poetic qualities itself, nor is it necessary to poetry" (C. Wheeler, *The Design of Poetry*, p. 209), but that it is nevertheless a very common poetic device, widely used by Hugo himself.

Most of the poems cited by Peyre are composed of alexandrines or twelve-syllable lines. Often within the same stanza are found classical alexandrines (with four stressed syllables—one at the end of each hemistich and one within each hemistich) and romantic alexandrines with only three stressed syllables (with the "coupe ternaire"):

> e.g.: *Ah! La philosophie est vorace,* last stanza:
> Pas de pilóte; pas de boussóle; rêvér
> Dans tóut lointain nuáge une ríve abordáble,
> . . .

I decided from the start not to try to imitate Hugo's metrical pattern. First of all, the alexandrine, which is commonly used in French and which is perhaps the best suited to the genius of the French language, is less used in English where the iambic pentameter holds much the same place as the alexandrine in French. Secondly, the English alexandrine does not correspond exactly to the French twelve-syllable line in that it normally contains six accented syllables instead of three or four. Finally, in the case of the alexandrine as well as in that of the octosyllabic line, the introduction of a regular stress pattern in English would limit the choice of words, which might thus tend to be less "poetic" to meet the requirements of stress. I therefore opted for free verse, which does not have to follow obvious and usual patterns in meter and line length.

However, meter does have definite functions in poetry (cf. C. Wheeler, *The Design of Poetry*, pp. 233–38). Thus, while not following a strict metrical pattern, I nevertheless had to ensure

that the major functions were fulfilled by other means. One of
the primary functions of meter is to add "otherness" to a poem,
an extra artistic dimension not found in normal, everyday language and life. The "otherness" normally provided by meter has
had to be furnished by various devices in my translation of Hugo.

The multiplication of interjections and vocatives:

e.g.: *Sous terre / In the grave*, Stanza 1:
—Laisse-moi. — Non. — O griffe sombre,
Bouche horrible! ô torture! ô deuil!

— Leave me alone. — No. — Oh, sinister claw!
Oh, yawning jaws! Oh, torture! Oh, sorrow!

The constant choice of formal and literary words and structures:

e.g. 1: *Satan pardonné / Satan Forgiven*
Oh! l'essence de Dieu, c'est d'aimer. L'homme croit
Que Dieu n'est comme lui qu'une âme, et qu'il s'isole
De l'univers, poussière immense qui s'envole;...

Oh! The essence of God is love. And man believes
That *God is but a soul* like him, and that he *stays aloof*
From the universe, that tremendous dust which flies away;...

e.g. 2: *Satan pardonné / Satan Forgiven*
Et ce coeur dans son gouffre a l'infini, moins un.
Moins Satan, à jamais rejeté, damné, morne.
Dieu m'excepte. Il finit à moi. Je suis sa borne.
Dieu serait infini si je n'existais pas.

This heart embraces the infinite, with one exception.
This exception is Satan, *eternally* rejected, damned and de-
jected.
God excludes me; *I mark the confines of his kingdom.*
God would be infinite if I did not exist.

The heightening of imagery:

e.g. 1: *Satan pardonné / Satan Forgiven*
Dieu m'excepte. Il finit à moi. *Je suis sa borne.*
God excludes me; *I mark the confines of his kingdom.*

e.g. 2: *Satan pardonné / Satan Forgiven*
Et c'est l'étonnement des espaces sans fin
Que ce coeur, blasphémé sur terre par les prêtres,
Ait autant de *rayons* que l'univers a d'êtres.
(...)
Splendide, il aime, et c'est par reflux qu'on l'adore.

And to the great astonishment of all,
This loving *sun*, blasphemed on earth by priests,
Has as many *rays* as there are beings in the universe,
(...)
Resplendent, he loves and is adored in return.

Here the image of God as light is pushed further than in French.

By these and other means, I have tried to create the "otherness" associated with poetry, the "otherness" to which meter normally contributes.

These, then, are the choices I have made regarding the translation of Hugo's works, and more particularly his poems. If one considers the overall options I have selected in light of the three approaches to the translation of poetry presented by Albert Schneider in "La traduction poétique" (*Meta*, 23:1 [March 1978], 20–36), my translations fall into the second category of *"Übertragung ou mieux, Nachdichtung"*. According to Schneider, the first category (which he calls *"Übersetzung"*) includes faithful, rather literal translation that makes no claims to artistic ambitions; the third (which he calls *"Umdichtung"*) covers a brilliant but not necessarily faithful rendering of the original, in true poetic form; and the intermediate category, into which I fall, covers the gamut ranging from the faithful translation of poetry into elegant and even poetic prose (*Übertragung*) to the faithful and beautiful transposition of poetry into verse (regular or free, rhymed or unrhymed) in the target language (*Nachdichtung*).

While I cannot claim to have reached the stage of "*Nachdichtung*", I feel I have gone beyond "*Übertragung*", for I have retained verse form and tried to add some elements of rhyme in the most general sense. And while it would have been a great achievement to have produced a true "recreation" of Hugo's poems, I believe that Hugo's texts as I have translated them meet the purpose for which they were intended quite adequately. Henri Peyre has cited passages from Hugo primarily to indicate the romanticist's ideas—this is clearly shown by the fact that the extracts at the end of the work are grouped by subject matter; therefore, a faithful prose translation might have sufficed. But Hugo's ideas are indissociably intertwined with his style; thus, although Peyre's intention in citing Hugo is to present Hugo's philosophy, I felt that considerable attention needed to be paid to the artistic elements of the writer's works. Finally, in attempting to reproduce, at least to some extent, some of Hugo's stylistic devices, I have borne in mind the expectations of those who are likely to read this work: they will undoubtedly be connoisseurs of literature, who will demand more of the translations of Hugo than bare facts and mere ideas.

In conclusion, I will ask the readers to remember as they peruse this work that the task of a translator is never an easy one, since it takes into account the intents of the primary source (the author) and of the secondary source (the translator), the message in terms of both form and content, the medium used to transmit the message, and finally the reaction of the receptors of the text in translation.

VICTOR HUGO

ONE

LIFE

Victor Hugo spoke about himself often in both his poetry and his prose works, recalling his childhood memories and embroidering on them, excusing and perhaps explaining the successive, contradictory, and sometimes confusing stages in the evolution of his sensibility, ideas, and political attitudes. Much research has been done on his life and loves by biographers, some of whom were not very favorably inclined towards him, and by a few hagiographers. But Hugo revealed much less of his true self than other romantics. He did not disclose his innermost thoughts and feelings in private diaries or letters. He lived a full life, but he lived mainly for his work, and it is in his work that one should look for the profound repercussions that events had on him and for the main elements of what can be called his position with regard to great philosophical, religious, and moral problems, which constitutes more particularly the subject of this study.

Victor Marie Hugo was of peasant stock, and perhaps this was the reason for his physical strength, which astounded his close relatives once he had got through his earliest years when the survival of a child as puny as he seemed doubtful. His father, who came from eastern France, became a general and a count during the empire. Hugo has described his mother as a "native of Vendée"; however, although she did come from the west of France, she had not espoused the antirevolutionary cause at all. She has been shown to have been liberal in politics, Voltairian in religion, and very distrustful of Catholicism, but with a romantic turn of mind. She willingly harbored conspirators during the empire, the most important one being Victor Lahorie, her lover, an officer involved in a plot to kill Napoleon, who took part in a second conspiracy when the emperor was in Russia and was executed. Hugo's two brothers, Abel and Eugène, were born in 1798 and 1800; Victor, born in 1802, was the youngest of the three. Much has been said about the guilt feelings that might have plagued the future great poet, who, as of an early age, surpassed his brother who had the unfortunate name of Abel and who was also a gifted person and a writer for some time. Charles Baudoin, who has attempted to psychoanalyze the poet after his death, has pointed out how often the character of Cain is found in his poems. The poem *La Conscience,* in which the eye of the assassinated brother looks at the guilty brother from the depths of the tomb, is a well-known work. In his long poem *Dieu,* Hugo generalizes by saying: "There is always a Cain to kill an Abel." The theme of brothers who are enemies, a common theme in many Greek tragedies, is found once again in the poems and in a few plays of Hugo (*Les Burgraves*). Perhaps the youngest of the three sons was the cause of some jealousy on the part of his older brothers, as he was their rival for the affection of their mother. In fact, it was Eugène who was privately jealous of his younger brother, since he was secretly so in love with the latter's fiancée, Adèle Foucher, that he lost his sanity on the same day that Victor and she got married.

The poet has lavishly used memories of his childhood in his poems and has presented this period of his life as a veritable Eden. No doubt this is how Hugo the adult saw his childhood. Actually, however, there was little peace in the Hugo family. During a stay in Corsica in 1803, Hugo's father had established an intimate relationship with a young woman called Catherine Thomas, who, as of that point, followed him everywhere and was flaunted by him as his mistress, while Mme. Hugo, thus made to look ridiculous in the eyes of everyone, was painfully humiliated.

The latter had quite a fierce nature, was very strict with her sons (who nevertheless adored her), and was motivated by an implacable hatred for her husband. There were always quarrels and recriminations when husband and wife were together, even in front of the children. Mme. Hugo died in 1821, and the general immediately married his mistress. The father, who was often away from home, had very little influence on the future poet. Hugo retained only delightful memories of a few glimpses of Spain, where the family had gone to join the father who was then stationed there. Raising the children was left to the mother.

In-depth research, particularly that done by Chanoine Géraud Venzac, has shown that Mme. Hugo flatly refused to give her sons a religious upbringing. Apparently, Victor was not baptized, or he was baptized only very late in life, on the advice of his father and with the friendly help of Félicité Lamennais, in order to obtain a marriage certificate. In Spain Mme. Hugo had her children registered as Protestants so they would not have to participate in prayers and ceremonies of the Catholic ritual. Victor Hugo, who became deeply religious in his adulthood and who was an assiduous reader of the Bible, never studied catechism and did not take his first communion. At first he was Voltairian; then, between 1820 and 1826, he became a Christian and, simultaneously, a royalist. In 1827 his interest in Christianity, which was then purely nominal, flagged, and his weak royalism gave way to the cult of Napoleon. In his earlier poems, he sometimes spoke ill of Voltaire. Later, at the time he wrote Les Misérables, he praised him highly, as Alphonse de Lamartine had done in his Histoire des Girondins, when he, too, moved away from Catholicism.

Victor Hugo made a brilliant start in literature. As early as 1810 he had written: "I want to be Chateaubriand or nothing." It is interesting to note, however, that his enthusiasm for this predecessor of romanticism waned after he visited him, when Hugo was about twenty-two, and found his ideal haughty and aloof. As early as 1819, the young poet had received a prize at the *Jeux Floraux* of Toulouse and started a literary review. His *Odes* appeared in 1822, four months before his marriage to Adèle Foucher, the daughter of family friends. The *Lettres à la fiancée*, published much later, show the great purity, idealistic passion, and adoration of woman found in his love. The young couple was poor. A first child died a few months after birth; Léopoldine was born in 1824; then came Charles in 1826, François-Victor in 1828, and Adèle in 1830. These pregnancies wore out the young wife. But as of 1827, her husband had made his mark and was accepted as the leader of the new literary school. Odes, ballads, colorful images of an imaginary Orient, topical poems, and finally the two works that made him well known, *Hernani* in 1830 and *Notre-Dame de Paris* in 1831, following a few outlandish novels, made Hugo famous but also won him the jealousy of several of his friends from earlier days. M. Charles Sainte-Beuve wormed his way into Mme. Hugo's life, courted her and became her lover, and immediately increased the reservations he expressed about his rival and the barbs he directed against him in his articles on him. Hugo, who up to that point had sincerely loved his wife, became Juliette Drouet's lover in 1833.

After several abortive attempts, Hugo was finally elected to the French Academy at the age of thirty-nine. Despite his fame, the diversity of his inspiration (which could not be matched by other romantic poets), and a creative fecundity surpassed only by Honoré de Balzac, Hugo felt overwhelmed by the feeling of melancholy that overtakes middle-aged men. He recognized the danger of all lyricism—the monotony of an inspiration that constantly dwells on itself, the difficulty of making relatively short poems and songs compete with the epic and its nineteenth-century successor, the novel. His theater is much better than has been indicated by critics who carried their discretion to the point of pusillanimity, but Hugo thought that extravagant lyricism or unrestrained local color was not consonant with the psychological drama the French wanted to revive at that time. As he grew more mature, he became more interested in social questions that appealed to a so-called bourgeois society that, however, was secretly afraid of the fatal consequences of the industrial revolution. He dreamed of being a leader of men, as Lamartine had been, and of improving the lot of the underprivileged and the workers, as Jules Michelet wished to do. In 1845 he began the work *Les Misères,* which became *Les Misérables* twenty years later. The same year, Louis-Philippe, who at first was only slighty interested in the poet—one of whose plays (*Le Roi s'amuse*) he had formerly banned—raised Hugo to the peerage. This honor was of some help to Hugo when he was caught redhanded committing adultery with an attractive and interesting woman, Mme. Biard, in July 1845. As a peer of the realm, he was inviolable; it was she who had to go to prison.

On September 4, 1843, while Hugo was traveling with Juliette Drouet in the southwest of France, his daughter, who had recently married Charles Vacquerie, drowned accidentally in the Seine, at Villequier. Hugo was crazed by grief, as he indicated in a poem. Claire, who was Juliette Drouet's daughter by the sculptor James Pradier and whom Hugo loved like a father, died in 1846. His two sons got typhoid. The honors he received in the political activities he was involved in did very little to brighten the gloom that Hugo felt developing within him. He had become a poet of darkness and was obsessed by death and what might be beyond it.

Then came the Revolution of 1848. The political role of the former peer of France (the Upper House had been abolished by one of the first decrees of the provisional government) was ambiguous during the years 1848–51. The contradictions in his attitude and the compromises he made have been brought out with unwarranted malice. No doubt the poet who had become a prophet anticipated playing a major role, possibly by working with the Rightists or the Republicans, or even by supporting Louis-Napoleon, who a few years before had seemed to be a noble adventurer and had advocated the abolition of pauperism.

The choice depended on the time, on events, and on the wavering attitude of the poet, whose political ideology was never very consistent in those troubled times. In 1851 at least, Hugo rose all the more indignantly against Louis-Napoleon, as the poet himself had to bear part of the responsibility for the diffusion of the Napoleonic myth. Hugo decided to play an active part in resisting the coup d'état of December 2, 1851. His two sons were thrown in prison, but he escaped to Brussels. One of the first of Napoleon III's decrees concerned his exile. On August 5, 1852, Hugo took refuge in Jersey, but he was soon banished from this island, and in 1855 he went to the neighboring, more desolate island of Guernsey, where he lived until the empire collapsed.

For a long time, to the middle of the twentieth century, it was the poems written before Hugo's exile that were part of the school curriculum and were recited by hordes of children; it was thanks to them that Hugo had in fact become the first French poet to be popular with all social classes. If he had disappeared from the scene in 1851, he would certainly have retained his reputation as the most talented of the poets of his century. But he would not have been known for his philosophy. For it was after his exile, which he knew had been good for him and which he missed at times after 1871, that he became the profound and truly great poet that he was, haunted by the deepest metaphysical and religious problems.

To be sure, he had already shown himself to be a poet of reverie and a visionary in *Les Feuilles d'automne* (1831), and many of the poems found in the collections that followed were contemplative in nature. But the splendor of his imagery, his gift for the picturesque, his effects of light and shade (which were worthy of the two painters he appreciated the most, Dürer and Rembrandt), and the lyrical eloquence of his plays had taken precedence for a while over the role of "dreamer" and "thinker" that he assumed after 1853. Before reaching this stage, he had known much sadness. There is a disturbing item scribbled in his notebooks and added into the work *Post-scriptum de ma vie*, published in 1901; according to two of the men who best judged the poet, J.-B Barrère and H. Guillemin, this note contains an allusion either to his wife's betrayal of him or to her coldness:

Woe betide him who loves without being loved!
Oh! It's a dreadful situation. See this woman.
She is charming. She is sweet and pure and ingenuous. . . .
But she does not love you. It is not that she hates you.
But she just does not love you.

Hugo was discreet enough never to display in his poems the sorrows connected with his love life. In any case, his extraordinary capacity for physical love and his eager pursuit of women from very different walks of life brought him some compensation. He forgave himself for his carnal frailties and even for the pain he thus caused Juliette, who was frequently abandoned for younger and often vulgar women. But as a result, he was all the more convinced that man is basically evil and should pray for forgiveness.

Hugo had also known remorse. He confessed his failings to a few friends, and, like Rousseau, he consoled himself with the thought that by regretting them he was better than others. He confessed in 1830 that his Catholicism, which had never been an intimate part of his life, had lost its religious and poetic fervor. He added that he had stopped praying at that time. His involvement with convicts and criminals unjustly treated by society and the fluctuations in his political views served to hide his latent tendency to feel distressed by the idea of death and the possibility of the nothingness after it. For about ten years following the death of his daughter, the grieving father reflected slowly but surely on life after death and communication with the dead. He rebelled against the nihilism of death. In *Paroles sur la dune,* Hugo wrote: "How similar memories are to remorse!"—a cry that André Gide, a harsh critic, considered the most Baudelairian of all the poet's laments. He confessed to having strange forebodings and to believing in superstitions his friends might have considered puerile.

Suddenly, once he was in Jersey, facing the depths of the ocean and faced with his solitude, listening to the storms raging, looking at the trees contorted by high winds, surrounded by exiles venting their rancor against the imperial régime and dreaming impossible dreams, Victor Hugo discovered new sources of inspiration within himself. After his scathing attack against the "usurper," *Napoléon le Petit*, which put an end to any hopes of his being allowed to return to France, he published, at the end of 1853, *Les Châtiments*, comprising the most venomous and monumental lyrical satires probably ever written in any language. Certain extracts from *L'Expiation*, inevitably found in most anthologies, could well seem boring to the French today. However, the complete work is characterized by both moving and dazzling oratory and force.

About the same time, Mme. de Girardin, a friend who paid a visit to the Hugo family, introduced them to "table turning," which was then a novelty in Europe. At first Hugo was skeptical about it. However, his son Charles was extraordinarily gifted as a medium. His daughter Adèle, who was high-strung and unbalanced and who later lost her sanity after a crazy adventure in the New World, revealed some strange points concerning the mysticism of her father in the diary that she kept during the period of exile. Hugo was finally convinced about the reliability of table turning after the death of his daughter, when her spirit was conjured up by the medium and seemed to reply in person to those questioning her and to bring a message from beyond. He resorted constantly to table turning and conjured a whole series of great men, including Shakespeare, whose works were then being translated by his son François-Victor. In all good faith, Hugo inspired their responses and heard them confirming his philosophical and sometimes political and literary views.

Nervous tension ran high among all who attended these séances; one of them even went mad. At night the poet, who frequently suffered from insomnia, was visited by the "White Lady" and other ghosts about which the superstitious inhabitants of the island had spoken to him. He feverishly composed philosophical meditations, apocalyptic prophecies, and esoteric epics presenting the transmigration of souls and the purification of the wicked by charitable forgiveness, and he attributed long passages in his works to God, Christ, and the Devil. Thus he replaced what he considered implacable and narrow-minded in Christianity by a religion that, while retaining Christianity's best aspects, would go beyond it. About half of *Les Contemplations* (a collection of poems, many of which had been written before 1853, published in 1856), *Dieu, La Fin de Satan,* and two or three other volumes, most of which were not completed and were published only after the poet's death, were written during these months of feverish inspiration, as was also many a page of prose.

The poet was in danger of becoming mentally disturbed from nervous wear-and-tear and could have lost his mind. His doctors advised against his seeking spiritualistic revelations. The only thing that saved the exiled giant, whose health could so easily have given way, was his strong constitution, for his senses, appetite, and resistance to an inclement and hostile climate were as much above the average as his sexual vigor and his imagination. The table-turning experiments were stopped. The accounts of Hugo's conversations with the beyond, preserved by the poet himself, were published after his death. Claudius Grillet, Auguste Viatte, Jean Gaudon, and other scholars have studied them with respect. No doubt the bizarre speculations of the poet and metaphysician were influenced to some extent by recollections of what he had hastily read (Hugo preferred seeing to reading) and of what had been said by a few of his visitors who had long been attracted by irrationalism or esotericism. But like Molière and Goethe, Hugo used as he pleased dictionary entries or the few book references he happened to come across. His ideas were very much his own, and they were a result of his anguish, of his desperate need to believe in something, and of his conviction that morals, history, and politics all had to have a meaning that lay beyond the confines of human life.

This was undoubtedly what Hugo had in mind when he proudly rebelled against death. He was always naïvely egocentric and convinced of his greatness as a writer and even as a diviner. His family, who were then often inclined to be sick and who were getting impatient about the prolonged exile, provided Hugo with fresh and rich sources of inspiration. Even when Napoleon III instituted a more liberal régime and in 1859 granted amnesty to those exiled, the poet, in his pride, preferred to remain on his rock, alone if necessary, refusing to compromise his principles. In 1865 his wife and two sons settled in Brussels; Mme. Hugo died there on August 27, 1868. But even before his exile, Hugo had proclaimed his faith in the triumph of life-after-death over death, on occasions when he had been invited to speak at funerals or at centennial celebrations. On August 20, 1850, at the funeral of Balzac, whom very few of his literary colleagues knew or dared really to admire at that time, Hugo, with great clear-sightedness, had classed this extraordinary novelist, in spite of his often conservative opinions, among "the courageous breed of revolutionary writers." He added in serious tones:

> Such deaths prove immortality. When faced with the death of certain famous men, we are more clearly aware of the divine destiny of that spirit that comes to earth to suffer and be purified, that spirit which is called man, and we feel that those who were geniuses during their lifetime cannot fail to survive after death. (*Actes et Paroles*, vol. I)

When his publisher, Hetzel, discouraged the poet turned prophet and metaphysician from publishing his apocalyptic works *Dieu*, *La Fin de Satan*, and *L'Ane*, as they would not be appreciated by the second-empire public, which was down-to-earth, prosaic, and prudently orthodox, Hugo began to write his "short epics," which were published in 1859 under the title of *La*

Légende des Siècles. This collection was for a long time Hugo's most popular poetic work, and it probably still is today. It consists of poems that are less mystifying than the later poems of *Les Contemplations,* which bordered precariously on the infinite. Narrative poems, written with vigor and tremendous virtuosity, and more intimate poems, filled with pity for the poor, outcasts, and animals, are found side by side with other poems such as *Le Satyre* and hymns to the future and to peace among nations, which reintroduced philosophy in the epic. Hugo was not at all afraid of confusing his reading public. He knew that great and even serious men can laugh on occasion, that Aristophanes, Luther, Rabelais, and even Balzac had been able to combine truculence and mysticism, winged fantasy and moral satire. It took a lot of courage for him to publish the licentious *Chansons des Rues et des Bois* in 1865, at the very moment when he had astounded his public with revelations made by spirits. There was a Dionysian, erotic, and faunlike aspect to his nature. He preferred to display it unrestrainedly rather than suggest it in a refined manner as other sensualists such as Mallarmé and Valéry later did. Just as true religion is not solely concerned with the tragic aspect imputed to it by men like Pascal, so also poetry is not solely connected with melancholy or conveyed by sibylline prose. J.-B Barrère has judiciously and skillfully shown the whole side of the genius of the poet that can be appreciated and studied under the heading "Flights of imagination."

But the most important event in Victor Hugo's career between the publication of *Les Contemplations* and his return from exile was the completion of *Les Misérables* and its publication in five parts in 1862. Since about 1930, when interest in Hugo greatly increased, even the most supercilious of critics have given up the absurdly disdainful attitude of their predecessors towards this novel, intelligible to, written for, and enjoyed by the common reader. *Les Misérables* is by no means a novel that can be considered a model of literary technique, as *Madame Bovary* was by the disciples of Flaubert; nor does it contain a model of subtle psychology, such as the followers of Stendhal found in Henri Beyle, whom Hugo detested as much as Claudel did later. Yet this vast epic written in the form of a novel remains the most widely read French novel of the last century. Several parts of *Les Misérables* (the famous "Tempête sous un crâne," the pages devoted to prayer, faith, and poverty, the idea of a "philosophical preface") make it a great philosophical novel as well as a social novel— perhaps the only successful one of its kind, for this genre tends to be an ambitious one and abounds in failures.

William Shakespeare (1864), which was the other great prose work written by Hugo during his exile and whose digressions and enumerations it was formerly considered in good form to find amusing, has also had its reputation restored. To be sure, one cannot hope to find in it irrefutable interpretations of Shakespeare's plays, although some of the observations on *Hamlet* are the most searching that have been presented since those of Goethe in *Wilhelm Meister*. But the book contains a great number of ideas dealing with Shakespeare's literary works and his personal philosophy, and it also presents an indirect portrait of Hugo, which cannot be ignored in any study, however general, of Hugo's philosophy.

Victor Hugo continued to write many poems after his great period of poetic creation from 1853 to 1859. Some of them, published in the collections *Toute la Lyre* and *Les Quatre Vents de l'Esprit,* and in the various notebooks entitled *Océan* or *Tas de Pierres,* are considered to be among the finest examples of Hugo's creative genius. He also continued to compose plays after he had seemingly given up the theater, following *Les Burgraves. Torquemada* (1882) is a gripping play, and the *Théâtre en liberté,* freed from the restraints of stage performance, anticipates a whole series of modern experiments to restore liberty, imagination, and life to the theater. But Hugo's ideas and his gift as a visionary are best revealed in three great novels. It seems to be generally recognized today by the discerning that it is not at all degrading to admire something that is also appreciated by a wider public, which likes to be deeply moved. To be sure, these novels have their faults, but so do those of Dickens, Tolstoy, and Dostoevski. What is most important, however, is that these novels of Hugo's are instinct with life. In addition, they are fraught with ideas, in their own way. These novels are *Les Travailleurs de la Mer* (1866), inspired by Hugo's sojourn on the Anglo-Norman islands, *L'Homme qui rit* (1869), perhaps the most outstanding French visionary novel, and *Quatre-Vingt-Treize* (1874).

Through the years, Hugo had become increasingly opposed to organized religions, which he considered as too conservative and complacent about their lack of true charity, and to useless wars and conflicts between civilized nations. The 1870 war and the implacable attitude of the conquerors toward defeated France was as sad an awakening for him as it was for Michelet and Renan. Hugo returned to France immediately after the fall of the empire on September 4, 1870. He made many eloquent appeals to the Prussians, the French, and the Parisians. He was elected to the National Assembly in February 1871, but he did not consort easily with the politicians. During the Commune, he happened by mere chance to be in Brussels because of the sudden death of his son Charles. After being defeated in the elections of July 1871, Hugo stayed away from active politics. He considered his election to the Senate five years later only as one of those honors that consecrated his glorious career in the last years of his life and that he readily accepted. He had joined the Republican party quite late and, as he explained in a letter to Alphonse Karr in 1869, the reason for his joining was "to side with the weaker party." The party had won the day. Thus Hugo presided at conferences, received the homage of many foreign visitors, lavished words of encouragement and faith in the future, and intervened on behalf of former Communards who had been convicted. A few works dating back to an earlier period were published at this time—*Le Pape* (1878), *La Pitié suprême* (1879), *Religions et Religion* (1880). As of 1878, the year when he had suffered a stroke, and even more after the death of Juliette Drouet on May 11,

1883, Hugo seemed to be awaiting death. He died on May 22, 1885. He was given a magnificent state funeral, which was recorded for posterity in the literature of that period. His reputation suffered for some time, when the poetry of the young Symbolists seemed to repudiate his own. However, Mallarmé had always respected him, and he reproved his young disciples, according to Claudel, who was one of them, if they ventured to show lack of deference for Hugo. Claudel himself, Aragon, Rostand, and Verhaeren were not really all that different from Hugo, even though they were sometimes amused by him.

It is true that the generation following Hugo's had moved away from what it considered flatulence of style or verbal delirium, for it wanted, for a while, to kill eloquence, just as Hugo himself, at a much earlier date, had declared "war against rhetoric." Such periodic reactions are healthy, although it is doubtful whether true poetry can do without any eloquence whatever, if it has its source in a strong inspiration and seeks to make others share in the poet's vision. But if Hugo has regained the admiration of critics and readers since about 1930, it is not only because of his extraordinary mastery of the language and his imagination, but also because of his ideas and the originality of his philosophical intuitions. Yet Émile Faguet, who sometimes read hastily and unmethodically, had foolishly accused Hugo of not having thought deeply.

Later, others who were far less reputable than Faguet, obsessed as they were by their political conviction that democracy was the root of all evil, accused Hugo of having been nothing but "the pundit of demagogy." However, the poet, who was prone to immoderation and ready to plunge into chaos, confident that he could bring beauty and order out of it, was never afraid of laying himself open to criticism. "It is wonderful to be open to attack," he declared in *William Shakespeare*. He sometimes caused people to smile or laugh, and he could, when necessary, laugh heartily at himself. He knew also how to retain his faculty of reasoning as he plumbed the depths of the irrational. But his reflections have often drawn aside the curtain veiling the mysteries of life, whereas the less adventurous prefer merely to gaze at the curtain rather than to look beyond it. If France can boast of any great philosophical poetry, it is probably Hugo's rather than Ronsard's, Vigny's, or Valéry's.

TWO

———————◆———————

PHILOSOPHY

Excellent poets, who have reflected a great deal and had original ideas, have found that it is impossible to write philosophical poetry. Valéry considered it an artificial, hybrid genre, almost impossible to use successfully; in fact, according to him, the only one to succeed in this genre was Lucretius. In England, T. S. Eliot, discussing the stoicism of Seneca, dared to ask a question that is sheer blasphemy for an Anglo-Saxon: "Did Shakespeare ever have any ideas?" His answer was that the author of *Hamlet*, like all poets, aimed only at expressing "the emotional equivalent of ideas." In another, more famous essay, Eliot went even further: "It became obvious to me that if a poet wants to be a philosopher, he should virtually be two men, and I know of no examples of such schizophrenia. Moreover, I see no advantage in such a combination. For the task is better accomplished in two brains than in one."

It would be easy to respond to Eliot's declarations by saying that such schizophrenia has characterized many poets who, like Saint Paul or Faust, have felt the presence of two souls in conflict within them, and that, in the case of Victor Hugo in particular, there are more than two men making their presence felt. Since the romantic period, the poetry written in various languages has been inspired by anxiety about the fate of man. It has expressed man's anguish with regard to the infinite and death, without always being able to dispel it. It has struggled with the dilemma

of reconciling fatalism with free will. It has tried to cut the
Gordian knot of the origin and ubiquity of evil. It has not been
able—and has not wanted—to remain indifferent to the moral
trials and social tribulations of a society that was rarely stable or
just. More than once since the French Revolution, it has advocated political involvement. Poets, in particular, soon felt the
need to widen the scope of lyricism and to vary its themes. Hugo
was inclined to assume the attitude of the "thinker" and the
"dreamer," and he was both, just as Goethe, Wordsworth, and
Shelley had been before him. In France, Vigny was not afraid to
call himself a poet-philosopher and to try an indirect, if not
impersonal type of lyricism in which philosophy, given flesh and
blood, would be incorporated. Lamartine was a far more profound philosophical poet than is generally believed (in *Jocelyn*
and *La Chute d'un Ange*) and no mean political thinker (in his
remarkable pamphlet on *La Politique rationnelle*); he himself declared, in a passage of his *Cours familier* of 1856, long after
having given up writing poetry, that "all poetry that does not
amount to philosophy is nothing but a bauble." Even earlier than
this, Baudelaire had written to his publisher Poulet-Malassis that
philosophy was everything. Finally, Hugo, in his notes for
William Shakespeare, rightly protested against the tendency to
consider poets as mere jewelers or embroiderers:

> Form and content. To say that form eliminates content, that,
> because there are images, there are no ideas, that, where there is
> poetry, there is no philosophy, is tantamount to saying that a
> scarlet Milet carpet is not a carpet, that a star is not a form of
> light, and that a beautiful woman is not a woman. . . .

We have long given up identifying consistency with truth,
depth with abstruse language, abstraction with sound judgment.
Well before the adjective *existential* became fashionable or the
word *dialectical* was used to glorify a philosophy, it was a recognized fact that philosophical sensibility expressed in a lively and

forceful manner and often through images has a more striking effect and gets its message across more clearly than a philosophy that is so rarefied and ethereal that it is understood only by specialists. For several centuries, more particularly in France, it was through literature that the educated public got to know philosophy.

This had a beneficial effect on literature itself in a country where it was in danger of attributing too much importance to style and a highly ornate style at that. Since the Age of Enlightenment (and since romanticism in the case of poetry), literature has generally been greatly concerned with religious, metaphysical, moral, and political problems. However, when discussing the philosophy of Hugo (or that of Goethe, Coleridge, or Claudel), it would be a mistake to try to systematize it too much and to present it in sections, using the headings of traditional textbook chapters. It should be conceded once and for all, from the start, that Hugo was no more afraid of contradictions than Plato, Pascal, Schelling, or Nietzsche were. Oftentimes, he was not even aware of them. In any case, many men who are far less imaginative than Hugo are not sure if they are Deists or pantheists, monists or Manicheans, if they are determinists or not, if their aggressive disbelief does not contain some hankering after lost faith, if they strongly believe in progress or think that pessimism is the best attitude to adopt when observing the world as it is today. It would also be a mistake to try to present the contradictions or, at least, the vicissitudes of pragmatic and therefore constantly changing philosophy as the result of a coherent evolution. It does not necessarily follow that the thoughts expressed and the weary attitude adopted late in life by Voltaire, Goethe, Schopenhauer, and Gide were better than what their minds had conceived of at the age of thirty or fifty. Sophocles's last plays, depicting the return of the blind Oedipus to Colonus, Titian's last paintings, and Stravinsky's last musical compositions do not necessarily present these great men's truest message.

As it happens, Hugo's great philosophical poetry was composed after he was fifty. However, his is an exceptional case, and the only other comparable one in this respect is that of Goethe. Even Valéry does not compare with Hugo from this point of view, for although he was in his fifties when he published *Charmes*, his philosophy had already been determined and formulated earlier. But Hugo's attitude did not change very much after his return from exile. When he reached his seventies, the poet agreed, in response to what seemed to be a national desire, to play the role of a spiritual guide, championing worthy causes and popularizing his philosophy of progress. So it was around the years 1853–65 that his imagination, obsessed by dismal visions, and his mind, craving for hope, found the molds into which could be poured a burning inspiration, stimulated by the questions to which the poet was desperately striving to find the answers.

THREE

THE PREEXILE PERIOD

Hugo did not wait until the age of forty to reflect on religious and philosophical problems or on the meaning of history. In his recollections and his evocations of the "Jardin des Feuillantines" and of his quick trips through Spain, he managed to romanticize his childhood. However, it was spent in the midst of the violent quarreling of his parents and in an atmosphere of hatred, scandal, and conspiracy. The young poet soon found recognition. But around him, men such as Joseph de Maistre, Ballanche, and Lamennais were striving to account for the excesses of the revolution, the adventures of the empire, and the history of mankind in general. The religiosity found in *Le Génie du Christianisme*, as well as the orthodox traditionalism that made a few young men praise royalism and Catholicism, did not really conceal the anxious doubts that had been left in people's minds by the theories of the eighteenth century. Chateaubriand himself was very Voltairian in many respects, and after 1830 Lamartine—rejecting the miracles and the Revelation, showing very little concern for redemption, and not being as obsessed by the image and message of Christ as Hugo, his junior, later was, or as Vigny was—had become a Deist and a disciple of Voltaire. *La Profession de foi du vicaire savoyard* had a long-lasting effect on the imagination of the romanticists. At one point, in the fourth poem of *Les Rayons et les Ombres*, Hugo cursed the skeptical irony of Voltaire,

that ape of genius
Sent on mission to mankind by the devil,

but he showed him more respect in Les Misérables. More and
more filled with admiration for the career and genius of Napoleon, he plied God and history with eloquent questions in his
attempt to understand why this "victor" had been vanquished
and what the plans of the Almighty, who alone controls the
future, were. But in his reflections on revolutions, at the end of
"Napoléon II" in Les Voix intérieures, Hugo only developed
platitudes in a rather facile manner. The doubts with which
Hugo struggled were better revealed in a few other poems found
in collections published before his exile.

Baudelaire spoke admiringly of Hugo's metaphysical curiosity,
that curiosity "of an Oedipus obsessed by many Sphinxes," in an
article written on June 15, 1861, and included after his death in
L'Art romantique. Baudelaire also recalled that, long before the
visions of the period of exile, a poem with metaphysical insights,
"La Pente de la rêverie," could have revealed to his contemporaries that Hugo was much more than a poet fascinated by the
play of forms and that his work was more profound than the
exotic splendor of Les Orientales leads one to believe. This
strange poem, included in Les Feuilles d'automne (1831), represents an incursion into the invisible. In a very simple tone, Hugo
begins with a description of the skyline of Paris in front of him,
and he goes on to an evocation of imaginary, chaotic worlds
that, before the dazzled eyes of the daydreamer, take over as the
real world suddenly vanishes. Drifting continents, lost cities,
walls and towers comparable with those of Piranesi, extinct races
along with the living, are all thrown together in this fantasy,
which seems to foreshadow Rimbaud's Illuminations. The
visionary is terrified by the sights thrust upon his inward eye. He
feels he is tottering on the brink of the abyss in the depths of
which he has "found eternity." However, reality and a familiar

background are still found in this bizarre poem, which is much too long and eloquent. This poem does not inspire quite so much terror in the reader as do the poems written during Hugo's great period. The poet, after having presented his vision of a universe in chaos, draws no conclusions and makes no daring conjectures. But the poem does contain the seeds of the theories that Hugo later ventured to express. Baudelaire, who reveals quite clearly in his poem "Rêve parisien" that he himself was no stranger to such visions, declared in his 1861 essay on Hugo that "every problem that was ever raised or tackled at any time by any philosophy has inevitably found its way into the poet's works."

Hugo's Roman Catholic faith, which had never been very profound and which had certainly not been instilled in him by his Voltairian mother or his nonreligious father, did not withstand the ideological movements that shook the literary and philosophical worlds to their foundations as early as the end of the Restoration. Lamennais was brought to the point of rebelling against orthodoxy. Théodore Jouffroy, after a night beset by doubts, rejected his earlier orthodox Christianity. Victor Cousin tried to reconcile the philosophies of various periods eclectically, and he was especially intrigued by the Neoplatonists and by the daring ideas of the Alexandrian school. The followers of Saint-Simon preferred to look to the future and proposed to modernists a rejuvenated faith, one better suited to the new working conditions and the new situation of entrepreneurs in a world to be reconstructed. Alfred de Vigny, Edgar Quinet, and Gérard de Nérval, when so moved, evoked the possible death of religion, of the gods and of God. Even Alfred de Musset, in the declamatory narrative poem *Rolla,* which he wrote at the age of twenty-three (1833), rejected the "Holy Writ" of Christ and hoped for a rejuvenation of those "old men born just yesterday," who were worn out before really having lived. "Which of us will become a god?" Men whose works Hugo read or glanced through and with whom he talked, men such as Pierre Leroux, dreamed of a humanitarian religion, and one less dogmatic and more sentimental and social than that formulated by Auguste Comte. In his introductory address to the French Academy in 1841, Hugo proclaimed his faith in God, which never faltered: "I believe in God and in Providence." But he also said, "I believe in mankind."

Even though Hugo believed in the existence of a supreme being, he did, nevertheless, have his moments of doubt, at least about that being's unfathomable plans and the reason for so many evils and distressing enigmas in God's work. Even before *Les Contemplations*, Hugo had wavered between doubt and affirmation. At times, he thought that all of nature had meaning and was bathed in light and prepossessing, as in "Spectacle rassurant," in *Les Rayons et les Ombres*; the voice of nature seemed to contrast with the mournful laments of man in "Ce qu'on entend sur la montagne," in *Les Feuilles d'automne*. But doubt used to build up within him, and thus, being torn asunder in his mind and heart, he was driven to despair. "That doubt is within us" is the title of one of the last poems of *Les Chants du Crépuscule*. He confided to a friend, Mlle. Louise Bertin, the uncertainty that he felt as a man who wanted to understand the true nature of things and who succeeded only partially, and he compared himself to a beggar longing to find a meaning to things, knocking at a door that remained closed. "Doubt! an ominous word, which I see written in flaming letters everywhere, in the dawn, in the lightning. . . ." In *Les Voix intérieures*, there is another poem addressed to the same friend, a much longer poem, whose title consists of two Spanish verbs: *"Pensar, Dudar."* For him, thinking means doubting. Everything is hazy; everything is vacillating. He feels that believing is no longer possible in this day and age, and yet man would like to regain his faith. "God built in no certitude in man. Thinking is not believing. . . ." The poet has examined nature very closely; he has asked it to reveal the secret it may be hiding; and at times it seems to want to speak to man. "But God forbids it." However, Hugo does not fathom the depths any further to attain certitude. He resigns himself to the inevitable more easily at this point than he will do later, after the tragedy at

Villequier:

> Since this is God's will, that's the way it should be.
> More light might blind our eyes. . . .

Hugo rarely quoted Pascal, the man who haunted Vigny's thoughts. Yet Hugo seemed to have borrowed Isaiah's reasoning concerning "the hidden god." According to the Jansenist, Pascal, we must accept the principle of God wanting to conceal the light from some while revealing the light to others. However, the conclusion of the poem *"Pensar, Dudar,"* in which Hugo tries to recommend resignation, lacks true conviction. "A Eugène Vicomte H.," the poem immediately following *"Pensar, Dudar,"* in the same volume of *Les Voix intérieures,* is more personal and moving. Hugo addressed it to his brother Eugène, who had lost his mind the day that Hugo got married in 1822, had been committed the following year, and had died on March 5, 1837, at the Charenton asylum. The poem begins with a series of "Puisque, puisque," whereby Hugo wants to submit to the unfathomable decrees of God. It continues with a touching evocation of their shared childhood memories. But the poet is soon beset by the presence of death, against which he secretly rebels. Yet looking lack on his life filled with strife and on the futility of human pleasures, he almost covets the peace found in death. In this emotional and melancholy elegy, there is no affirmation of immortality, no glimmer of victory over death that gives hope to the despondent poet, who had witnessed his brother's suffering for fifteen long years.

Between 1840 and the time of his exile, Hugo did not publish any more poetic works, although he did write a number of poems that were added to collections published during the period of exile and even later. He was busy with drama and, later, with politics and drafts of various novels. No doubt the poet continued to reflect on the nature of things, but his thoughts lacked the intense concentration later induced in the visionary by the solitude of his island and the extreme tension built up in his nervous system. His ideas on the major problems had remained confused, and he was well aware of this. In the well-known poem in which he recalls his memories of the Feuillantines period in about 1813, for the benefit of his own children gathered around him (Poem XIX in *Les Rayons et les Ombres*), he himself refers to the confused thoughts whirling around in his mind:

> My plans, my visions,
> My constant subjects of reflection,
> God, man, the future, reason, insanity,
> My schemes, a mass of shadowy, confused scaffolding. . . .

Hugo suffered a great deal during this period. His dramas were not a success; he was afraid that his inspiration might run dry; there was the tragic accident at Villequier; and he suffered from guilt and remorse over the scandal in which he was caught red-handed committing adultery with Mme. Biard, a scandal that had hurt Hugo the poet and peer much more deeply than he let on. All this urged him to seek answers to his questions more avidly. By the time he thought once again about publishing poems, after venting, in satirical lyrics, the monumental rage he felt against Napoleon III, Hugo had become a philosophical poet, a poet of darkness and of death, which he had to conquer or transcend at all cost. The chronology of the various poems he wrote at this stage is of little importance. They all deal often with the same distressing problems and present the hesitations, certitudes, and depths of his philosophy. It is certainly justifiable to attempt to synthesize this philosophy, provided the synthesis does not gloss over the contradictions and inconsistencies found therein and does not try to present the poet as a professional philosopher. It is no less justifiable to pass quickly over what are claimed to be Hugo's sources, which in fact are often purely hypothetical and imaginary—sources such as the French illuminists from Dom Antoine-Joseph Pernety, Fabre d'Olivet, and Pierre Ballanche to Eliphas Lévi; theorizers full of nebulous ideas such as Pierre Leroux, Jean Reynaud, and Alexandre Weill; gnostics; and interpreters of the occult. All Hugo needed to set in motion his mind, which hoarded proper names, and his imagination, which created myths, was a few snatches of conversation, a few dictionary entries.

FOUR

AFTER 1852: GOD

There was one point on which Hugo never wavered: the fact that God existed. He declared to several of his visitors and correspondents and to George Sand in particular on May 8, 1862: "I believe . . . in God far more than in myself. . . . I am more certain about the existence of God than I am about my own." But it is not clear what conception Hugo had of God, whether his God was that of the Christians or that of the Old Testament, or even the impersonal god of the Deists, that supreme watchmaker who set up the great mechanism of the universe, set it going with a flick of his hand—which Pascal derided in Descartes's work— and has rarely bothered about it since. Hugo did not express himself clearly on this point. He preferred to feel intensely and communicate the mystery of the divine impressionistically. Too much precision would be limiting and, furthermore, diminishing. Hugo could well have uttered Denis Diderot's admirable words: "Enlarge God!" In *Religions et Religion,* Hugo farcically attacked the pettiness of organized religions, which are often more inspired by primitive superstitions than by a purified faith and "which often belittle what God made great."

Hugo's god is certainly not the impersonal creator envisaged by the Deists, a god who, very prudently, stays aloof from the world, refuses to listen to prayers, and does not bother about guaranteeing us any form of immortality, or even of survival, after death. Nor is Hugo's god the one naively portrayed to

children, and sometimes even to adults, by a crude anthropomorphism, that god whom Xenophanes and, much later,
Voltaire poked fun at by suggesting that if horses conceived of a
god, this god must look like a horse.

Hugo declares that he does not believe in that "good old-
fashioned god," in a forceful poem of L'Année terrible, in which
he flares up at "the bishop who called me an atheist." In this
polemical epistle, whose forcefulness Charles Renouvier was one
of the first to point out, Hugo characterizes his religious experience. It is not that of a mystic, or even that of a Pascal, and
Jesus Christ is not the intermediary between Hugo and his god.
In fact, his religious experience remains abstract. But it anticipates Claudel's famous line on "someone who is within me and is
more myself than I am." Hugo declares that if God is

> The being whose soul lies deep within my soul,
> The being who speaks softly to me and constantly intercedes
> In favour of the true against the untrue... ,

then he is a believer. When all is said and done, Hugo's god is
rather similar to the voice of conscience heard by Rousseau and
Kant, an intimate and living form of moral law.

On the other hand, Hugo's god is not exactly (or, at least, not
invariably) the god of the pantheists, infused and diffused in
nature, controlling it and becoming one with it. Formerly, the
stoics, and Cleanthes in particular, and, later, poets such as
Goethe and Shelley found great poetic resources in this conception of the divine. There are pantheistic elements or expressions
in the works of many believers, who, however, disclaim this—in
the works of Claudel, for example, and in those of Teilhard de
Chardin, who liked to quote the famous words of the apostle Paul
(I Corinthians 6:28) announcing that once Christ's work is completed, "God will be all things to all men." Both protested
against asceticism, Christian as well as Buddhist, which had
totally condemned material things. Hugo too often exalted nature as being quasi-divine and inspired by a superior presence

and, at times, by an erotic quality. "God wants us to have been in love. Live and be envied," he cries to lovers in "Crépuscule" (*Contemplations*, II, XXVI). But, contrary to all logic, pantheism and faith in a personal god coexist in many people. "We are born of you," says Cleanthes to Zeus in his hymn, and St. Paul quotes this in his sermon on the Areopagus, presented in the Acts of the Apostles. Indeed, the naturalistic pantheism of the best poet among the ancient stoics had something in common with a Christian prayer.

Hugo's work provides no answers to the various questions posed by his very emotional and colorful philosophy. Indeed, there was no reason for him to write a catechism or a philosophy textbook. Did God create the world once and for all, assigning a fixed role to each entity within it and confining it forever within its laws? Did he provide for an evolution lasting for millions of years? Hugo does not bother to answer these questions or others. Darwin's evolutionism, as well as Lamarck's transformism at a much earlier date, had disturbed many poets, such as Lord Tennyson and Robert Browning in England. It did not shake Hugo's faith; the poet did not even feel the need to exclaim as Michelet did: "Give me back my own being!" Hugo considered evolutionism a form of materialism, and he rejected evolution as such, but his faith in God was in no way affected by it. In section XLIX of *La Légende des Siècles* (Poem X), Hugo, upholding his spiritualistic faith in man, that being who bears archangels' wings upon his shoulders, proudly rejected both Darwinism and nihilism, the latter being identified in his mind with German philosophy. Rather humorously—for Hugo certainly had a sense of humor—he concluded this rather nationalistic poem with the following lines:

And when a dignified, very proper, impeccably turned-out
  Englishman
Says to me: "God has made you a man, but I am making you a
  monkey.
Now, make yourself worthy of such a favor!"
This promotion makes me wonder a bit.

In fact, Hugo's attitude towards God, which was expressed in many different and, perhaps, somewhat contradictory ways, but which was based on some unshakeably solid convictions, cannot be categorized by any of the usual philosophical labels. In this, he resembles the majority of men, especially those who refuse to adopt an inflexible doctrine once and for all in the face of the many attractions of life. At certain times, Hugo was greatly attracted to polytheistic paganism, just as any man is who is struck by the multiple forces at work in the universe and who refuses to reduce them prematurely to a single cause. There has been much learned discussion of the grandiose poem *Le Satyre* and of the relative proportions of pantheism and monotheism found within it, but this kind of discussion is rather futile. Like any novelist or dramatist, Hugo assumed the role of the monstrous and mischievous rebel who was going to subjugate Jupiter, while he was composing this fervid philosophical epic. "Crépuscule," mentioned above, and ten other poems by Hugo would certainly be included in an anthology of nineteenth-century poems extolling the survival of the ancient gods, along with poems by Schiller, Hölderlin, Goethe, Keats, and Swinburne. Hugo slipped a few beautiful sentences, pregnant with meaning, into his *Promontorium Somnii:* "The pagan sees God as many-sided. His whole religion is protean. The pagan lives in suspense," and "Polytheism is the daydream haunting man." The awareness that Hugo had of mystery, of a Panlike eroticism aspiring to the divine in antiquity, owed little to erudition. He had drawn very little inspiration from Latin writers, with the exceptions of Vergil, Lucretius, and Juvenal. He knew Greek writers even less; Plato, Plotinus, Proclus, and Hermes Trismegistus were virtually unknown to him. But this was of little importance. His feeling for the ancient myths and for the fresh young imagination that had created them was more perspicuous than that of Leconte de Lisle, or even of Goethe, and that of many scholars. In *Promontorium Somnii,* he also alluded very perceptively to the tragic gloom that often veiled the Apollonian light, overvaunted by the Ancients:

> A strange light fell from Olympus on man, animals, trees, things,
> life and destiny. This halo was around all heads. It was delightful
> but disturbing, and sometimes cast a tragic ray.

Generally, however, Hugo could not be satisfied with longing
for the revival of the dead gods or with portraying, as the Parnas-
sians did, the successive religions in which mortals believed for a
while before giving them a royal burial or even going to the
point of spurning them by shattering their symbols. Following
Hegelianism and the reduction (by Creuzer and Quinet) of all
religions to a vast system of symbols, many philosophers of
Hugo's day took bitter pleasure in saying that all gods die, including God Himself, even if a vague sense of the divine continues to
exist. For Hugo, on the contrary, God continued to survive, and
with man's conception of Him purified, He was more resplendent
than ever. In *Le Tas de Pierres* (subtitled "Religion"), Hugo
noted:

> Religions are the garments that God is made to put on by man.
> These garments wear out. So the priests become panic-stricken.
> But they are wrong to do so. God still exists. Through the holes
> in the robe of religion, He can be clearly seen.

If Hugo had a keen sense of the multiplicity of a world in
which everything is in constant motion, is born and dies to be
reborn, with his antithetical turn of mind he was even more in
accord with the Manichean oversimplification whereby the
world is a battleground on which the forces of good and evil
come face to face. But once again, it would be imprudent to class
the poet in a specific category. For according to him, evil is not
coextensive with God. The universe is not divided between good
and evil. Manicheism is rejected in the long, unfinished poem
Dieu, in the section entitled "Le Corbeau." The ultimate victory
of the forces of good and of God, who pardons and accepts the

remorse of the archangel of evil, is never in any doubt. To be sure, the psychology of Hugo's characters in his novels and dramas is often simplistic, based as it is on a clear-cut distinction between the good and the wicked, the overbearing and the op- pressed. But the philosophy underlying these characters is by no means simplistic.

The essence of Hugo's god is love. This is stated by Satan at the end of the poem that Hugo devoted to him. Satan, the adversary, feels hated and rejected. But he knows that God does not remain aloof from the universe that he has created, that he is not indifferent to his work, which men have ruined:

> But I, the sad enemy and mocking, envious one,
> Know that God is not a soul but a heart.
> God, the loving heart of the world,
> Ties all the fibres of all the roots to his own divine fibres. . . .

However, this god who is love is not the god of the Christians, or at least not the god of the church. Hugo did not accept the principle of original sin, which St. Augustine, in developing his doctrines, read into an ambiguous sentence in the Epistle to the Romans (V,12). Moreover, Hugo did not seem to have been very impressed by St. Paul as a person. Nor did he subscribe to the Incarnation, the Trinity, the Resurrection, or the belief that the apostle Peter set up the papacy.

It is not clear whether Hugo's god reveals himself to man, and if he does, whether it is through the Decalogue, sacred books, prophets, or saints. Here again Hugo remains vague. He prefers to repeat in beautiful verses that God is absolute, unfathomable, and unknowable, and that philosophers have never succeeded in figuring out the mystery of the nature of the divine. He prefers to call himself a "dreamer," and the first of the voices heard in *Dieu* (section II) speaks to the "dreamer" that he is:

> Seeker, will you find what they have not found?
> Dreamer, will your dreams go beyond theirs?

A multitude of philosophical systems are presented, along with entire series of proper names, which Hugo was partial to. Plato, Locke, Lucretius, Swedenborg, Thales, Rousseau, Joseph de Maistre, and several others file past in a disorderly fashion before our eyes and warn the man given to asking questions to recognize his limits:

> Do not go beyond them. Seek God. But look for him
> In love and not in fear.

It is only in the hour of death that man can receive the revelation that he has anxiously been seeking all his life. Hugo's god, like Pascal's, is more sensitive to things of the heart than to things of the mind. It would be futile to try to prove this. Affirming it is more convincing for men like Hugo, who want to believe or, rather, who cannot help believing. "God's existence cannot be overemphasized," cried the poet, who was impervious to ridicule, in *Religions et Religion.* He alternately expresses anger at and pity for those who deny God, those fools who see nothing in the universe but "a vast monument to insanity."

> As their souls stir up the immense depths,
> They are not even aware of the universe,
> Within which the voice of God produces no echo. (*Pleurs dans la nuit*)

This god who is omnipresent is at the same time an entity apart from the universe he has created and this universe itself. All antinomies are integrated within him. He has a limited self, and yet he is the infinite, explained Hugo through the words of an old member of the Convention, on the point of death, in a strange passage in *Les Misérables* (I, 10). In this passage, Denis Saurat claimed to have detected a surprising similarity with the Zohar and the Cabala, though it is doubtful that there is any connection. Saurat was closer to the mark when he surmised, with complete deference to the esoteric philosophy of the poet,

that Hugo needed a god who was universal and free of any con-
straining religion, so to speak, and who was also, contradictorily,
a personal god, for Hugo, a fragment of the divine and endowed
with a strong personality, could only conceive of God as similar
to himself, also infinite in his own way. Indeed, in *Les Misérables,* Hugo reasons like a dialectician to prove that there are two
infinites, one outside us and another within us.

> It can be assumed that these two infinites are superposed, and
> that the second one underlies the first one. . . . If the two infinites
> are endowed with thought, each of them has a motivating force,
> and there is a self in the infinite above, as there is in the one
> below; the self in the infinite below is the soul, while that in the
> infinite above is God. (Part 2, "Parenthèse," V)

Like many other thinkers of his century, during which it was
considered inevitable to give up old religious formulas but essential to maintain the feeling and hope long represented by religion, Hugo did his best to provide a magnificent range of
synonyms for the word *god,* but he did not do this in the slightly
casual playful manner of men like Renan. Hugo had personal
experience of God, experience that he considered as irrecusable
as the sign that Pascal, the Jansenist, believed that he had received from Jesus Christ. Just like Pascal, Hugo, too, rejected the
god of the philosophers and scholars and preferred to pray to a
god who was responsive to human emotions. One of the "Rules
for the thinker," found in *Le Tas de Pierres,* states that the great
thinker is the one who retains a simple heart in the face of the
complications of the mind.

FIVE

———◆———

THE IMMORTALITY
OF THE SOUL

Although Hugo believed in the existence of God at least as much as he did in his own, and although he always rejected atheism as something incomprehensible to him, he certainly realized also that God is a necessary condition of immortality. As in the case of many other more systematic philosophers, his most intense thinking was inspired by death. Terror in the face of death and the resulting nothingness is by no means an edifying attitude. It is certainly more rational, as Montaigne soon discovered, not to steel oneself against suffering and death but to live life more fully as the end approaches and to resign oneself with a smile to the eternal laws. But not many mortals can emulate the noble courage of Spinoza, who calmly declared in his *Ethics* (IV, LXVII) that the wisdom of man is a meditation, not on death, but on life. Quite as intensely as Villon, Gautier, and Baudelaire, Hugo was aware of the physical aspects of death, of the body engulfed by water, eaten by worms, or reduced to ashes and to a few fleshless bones. He tried to believe, and at times to convince himself, that death leads to serene bliss, that death is a commencement, and he beseeched his reader, or the anxious interlocutor within him, to have faith: "Do not say 'to die'; say 'to be born'" (*Contemplations*, VI, XXII). In the same poetic work (VI, XIII, "Cadaver"), he extolled, as a pagan or a pan-theist might do, the return of the body to the earth, to flowers, to trees, to ravines, and to copses, all of which will be nourished by it. Poetically, he evoked this transformation of a living, thinking being into a harmonious element of immense nature:

And starlike, a new light shines forth in the lifeless eye.

However, there are many indications, in the last books of *Les Contemplations,* of moments of fright at the prospect of a possible void and moments of gloomy pessimism. *Pleurs dans la nuit* (Sections VI and XI) contains such unpleasant, gruesome pictures dealing with the decomposition of bodies that the poet has to beg God to forgive those he is chastising. At the end of this long lament, the poet, with a fresh burst of vitality, tries to dispel doubt and become "the universal voice of affirmation." To have something to bolster him up, Hugo needed to cling to the certitude that there was another existence, that the table-turning sessions did indeed reveal the fact that his daughter Léopoldine lived on after death. With humor mingled with great seriousness, Hugo wrote in *Post Mortem: Le Tas de Pierres:* "If there was no other life, there would be something dishonest in God." In other words, God owes us this. Without this, the dice would be loaded against us; without this, we would not be bound by moral law; without this, there would be no way to reward the righteous or to pardon and thus save the wicked.

Thus, Hugo considered that man had an implicit contract with God. In the same section of *Le Tas de Pierres,* he declared in a peremptory manner: "Our failings are debts contracted here and payable elsewhere. Atheism is nothing other than an attempt to declare insolvency."

So the argument is of a moral nature. God cannot treat us as well as Yahweh treated Job, who rebelled against the injustice in this world, and reduce us to our petty level in relation to the One who has filled the sky with stars. He owes us some reward, and he has to allow the wicked, for their own good, to expiate their sins in another life and to improve, perhaps through a series of transmigrations.

Hugo was not a philosopher by profession and was not expected to treat in a systematic fashion problems on which he preferred to express himself with heartfelt conviction. He was not required to give precise details concerning his conception of the immortality of the soul. Indeed, he did not indicate clearly whether this immortality, which he affirmed so strongly, was personal; whether it would be accompanied by the resurrection of the body; whether the faculty of thinking and feeling would continue to exist or be regained; whether a man worthy of being so called, in other words, a fighter, can, as Goethe hinted, be attracted by an afterlife containing no new hurdles; whether it would not be better to refuse sarcastically what Valéry described as that "dull and gilded immortality, . . . an empty skull and perpetual rictus." Obstinately, Hugo made man the starting point of his views on immortality. Man wants to be immortal; he feels deep down that he *is* immortal; he is endowed with free will. This last point was as indisputable a principle for Hugo as it is for Jean-Paul Sartre. If man is free to do good or evil, he is responsible. In the notes that he jotted down for his *William Shakespeare*—the key work that, he confided to a young visitor, Paul Stapfer, contained the secrets of his philosophy, which may well not be understood at first reading—Hugo declared that free will is the soul and that it implies resurrection, for resurrection involves responsibility. These matters are sacred mysteries, difficult to understand, but this did not impede Hugo, the firm believer, who, incidentally, preferred the stronger word *croyeur* to that of *croyant.* He had probably not read Kant, and he did not seem to worry about this. But his entire metaphysics was based on moral law, which is the only thread we have to hold on to as we wind our way through the labyrinth in which we are lost. "Sacrifice is a sign of immortality, since nothing finite can by itself explain sacrifice," Hugo wrote in "Reliquat," in *William Shakespeare.* An extract from *Le Tas de Pierres,* dated 1844 and presented like the preceding text in the second part of this book, already contained the following declaration: "He who proves the existence of God proves the existence of the soul. . . . Man is responsible" in terms of another life. "In death, man comes to an end and the soul comes into prominence." Without turning a hair, Hugo had given this passage the subtitle "On life and Death."

It is not clear whether this immortality will be granted to all men, or whether it will be granted to humans alone or to animals as well. Hugo does not evoke the traditional and childish image of paradise, in which thousands of millions of souls coexist in felicity, after having been allowed in by the Supreme Overseer. Although Hugo could very clearly see all angles of reality, he did not have a very clear picture, very fortunately, of afterlife. Hugo did not go as far as to insinuate, with a Renanlike smile, that he saw no reason for a Papuan to be immortal, and that this privilege is granted only to those who have developed full consciousness, for he had sided too often with the lowly and the underprivileged. But neither was he prepared to abdicate his role as a prophet and sage. His existence was conditioned by his belief in the triumph of the soul over death. This is what he indicated on the death of his son Charles in 1871: "If I did not believe in the soul, I could not survive even an hour longer." However, if there are men who refuse to believe in immortality, we can only be sorry for them. Without posing as a pundit, and with some humor, Hugo confided the following thoughts to young Professor Stapfer in 1868:

> I feel that I am immortal. If others do not feel the same way about themselves, I am sorry for them; but that is their business, for it is not up to me to question what they feel. No doubt they are right and they are not being misled by their instinct.

In a more serious tone, the poet expresses the same thought in verse, featuring Dante, in the fourth part of *Religions et Religion*, "Des Voix." According to him, there are great, wise, and very superior men, who include the giants of philosophy as well as the saints and the Indian ascetics, who, transfixed by their dreams, contemplate the supreme being (at the end of *Religions et Religion*):

> He has Conscience as his solstice,
> Justice as his axis,
> Equality as his equinox,
> And Liberty as his great dawn.

All these men, for whom God is overpoweringly present, know that they will have conscious immortality, a state into which they will pass directly at the time of death. The others, who will have only unconscious immortality, will have to go through reincarnation, dying and being reborn several times, before attaining final deliverance. (This is what Charles Renouvier indicated in his book *V. Hugo le philosophe*, pp. 254–58; and the same ideas were presented in *La Religion de V. Hugo* by Denis Saurat, who saw some resemblance between occult doctrines and Hugo's views on the subject of immortality.)

Hugo seems not to have studied Hindu philosophy as much as Lamartine, who enthusiastically read the *Ramayana* (*Cours familier de Littérature*, III, 1856), or as seriously as Leconte de Lisle or Jean Lahor. But Hugo's poetic imagination predisposed him to believe in Platonic reminiscence, in what he calls "prior memory," and in the occasional flashes of recognition that convince us that we have already lived through a particular moment in a particular place. So we are haunted by spectres of the past. At the end of the first volume of *Les Contemplations*, in "Autrefois" (III, XXX), Hugo has beautifully presented man climbing the ladder of creation, which is also the ladder of time:

> He has an unquenchable thirst;
> He feels other lives in his vertiginous past
> Coming to life again;
> He counts the attachments of his soul.

Deep down in the dark domes
He seeks the forms he has assumed;
He hears his own ghosts
Whispering to him from behind. . . .

And he says: "Death means knowledge;
We are groping our way out to the light.
I was, I am, and I am to be.
Death is a ladder. Let us ascend it."

Men less exceptional than the sages have perhaps not seen the light; or some failing has caused them to become too involved with material things and has led them away from God. The most guilty among them expiate their sins during the more lowly existences to which they are condemned. Oppressors, tyrants, embezzlers, and those Roman emperors whose monstrous crimes were clearly revealed by Suetonius and Juvenal; wives guilty of murder, like Delilah and Clytemnestra; petty critics, who are unmindful of great genius that is superhuman, and whom Hugo lashed out at through Zoilus, who disparaged Homer—all these beings have themselves woven the ropes with which they have been bound and whipped. A stirring passage in "Ce que dit la Bouche d'Ombre" evokes these criminals who are slaves to material things. But unlike Dante, Hugo is not happy, as a lover of justice, to condemn these cruel people to their infernal fate. Hugo has pity for all, and he begs for our compassion for all of them: "Have mercy. See souls in things. . . . Pity the prisoner, but pity the jailer." Some of these men have been metamorphosed into spiders, slugs, hideous crabs, and birds of prey. The proconsul Verres, who was denounced by Cicero,

Was a wolf in royal attire and is now a wolf in the forests.
Wide awake, he slides down the nightmare;
His laughter ends up as a howl in the depths of the woods.
Weep for what howls and weep for Verres.

While undergoing this punishment, which has forced his soul to enter the body of a so-called more lowly being, an animal, or to enter into material entities, the condemned creature suffers, but he does expiate his sins and draws closer to God. He can then opt for good and God and become a man again or, if he has totally repented, he can even become an archangel. In any case, this was what the poet had confided to Octave Uzanne, in *Propos de Table du poète en exil* (1892, p. 55). For Hugo, this belief in a kind of metempsychosis is not, entirely at least, a magnificent poetic prospect; for him, it is the expression of deep faith in an oft-affirmed animism and of great pity for all who suffer.

SIX

———————◆———————

PRAYER

In "Ce que dit la Bouche d'Ombre," the poem that is the key to Hugo's philosophy during the period of exile, and that was written during or shortly after the great crisis brought on by the revelations elicited by table turning (probably early in October 1854), Hugo forcefully declares that everything has a soul, that "consciousness pervades creation," that everything has meaning. Certainly, there were many men before Hugo, both occult philosophers and poets, who had believed things were instinct with life and, occasionally, with consciousness. Anthropomorphism abounds in the works of the so-called romantic poets, and the "pathetic fallacy," to use Ruskin's famous expression, is intimately linked with any sensibility that extends to things, however limited in fervor it may be. Lamartine timidly questioned those objects to which he was attached by moving memories:

> Inanimate objects, do you have a soul
> Which becomes attached to our souls
> And commands them to love?

Nerval, a Pythagorean on occasion, dreamed of eliminating the boundaries set up in the minds of the more conventional between conscious life and less conscious life, between men and trees and even rocks:

A pure spirit is growing under the rind of stones. (*Vers dorés*)

Hugo is even more daring, for he attributes to everything, including inanimate objects, "its own law, its own goals, its own path," a goal pursued semiconsciously, a familiarity with the path leading to it, and even a higher law obeyed by everything. There is constant dialogue between men and things. The wind, whose howling Hugo had listened to with intense fear in Jersey, and which he evoked as a blind, cruel, satanic force in a magnificent stanza of "Les Mages," is more than just a noisemaker in the revelation made by Rozel's spirit. "In the infinite, everything says something to someone." All that is necessary is to know how to listen and understand.

Prayer is the bridge between man and the Creator, the means whereby he can communicate with Him and intercede in behalf of the universe, which is endowed with a soul but not with speech. It is the role of the man who understands to interpret the vague signs made by the waves, the trees, the fields, and the glades. In this sense, God needs man as a link between His universe and Himself for the purpose of communication and intercession. The poet revealed to his young visitor, Stapfer, the great anxiety with which he sometimes awoke at night: "I feel that I can hear the groaning of a suffering soul, and this groaning haunts me until, by dint of fervent prayer, I have induced God to make it stop." For Hugo, praying was by no means a cowardly act, as it was for the stoic pessimist of *La Mort du Loup*. Nor was it a talisman, almost a superstition, or recourse to some form of magic, as it was for Baudelaire. Even Lamartine had declared that prayer was dead within him, after his daughter died in the Middle East, and God had no place in his work after 1832 or 1833. Hugo prayed constantly to a personal God, and not to Jesus Christ as Pascal and many mystics did. At times he begged God to accept his work as prayer. J.-B. Barrère, in his little book on Hugo in the series "Les Ecrivains devant Dieu," has presented a few moving sentences in which Hugo the family man advised his sons and his grandchildren to pray with conviction. On September 4, 1870—a strange coincidence—he made that sweet angel Léopoldine, who had died twenty-seven years earlier, the guardian of young Georges, whom he taught to clasp his hands to say grace. When begging God to take pity on his daughter Adèle, who was then committed for incurable insanity, he even went as far as to pray for divine pity for Louis Bonaparte after the fall of the empire. A beautiful passage on prayer, found in *Les Misérables*, is included elsewhere in this volume.

If, on the one hand, the tremendous egocentricity of Hugo the poet and prophet, and almost a fragment of God, is amusing (and rightly so), on the other hand, the humility that he sometimes displayed is very touching. He knew how to repent. He showed his remorse at that painful time when he went back to his wife in Paris, after having learned of the death of their daughter while he was on a journey with his mistress. His remorse was revealed once again when he, a peer of France, caught committing adultery with Mme. Biard, had to beseech his wife to intercede for the adulteress, imprisoned in accordance with the laws, and have her set free. Hugo never openly admitted that he believed in miracles. But he thought that God answers prayers and that He can change the course of things and take action to correct the plan He has set up from time immemorial, by what Malebranche called "particular acts of volition." For Hugo's heroes, such as Gilliatt in his heroic fight against the elements, and for the poet himself, prayer was far more than a prescription for moral health, good for increasing the strength of man, the fighter. Prayer could move God to pity. For Hugo, it was the sign of the constant conflict within him. For he was incapable of resisting carnal temptation and even betrayed Juliette with her own maid, but he was stricken with remorse and was ashamed of his sexuality in his old age, lust in his final years perhaps compensating for his continent and chaste youth.

SEVEN

CHRIST

Jesus Christ is certainly found in Hugo's works, as he is also in Lamartine's, Vigny's, and Nerval's, whereas there is little or no mention of him in the works of most of the English romantics and the German romantics after Friedrich Klopstock. The poem "Première Rencontre du Christ avec le tombeau," in the second section of the first *Légende des Siècles*, is a moving narrative evocation, but it does not attain the mysterious grandeur of the philosophical poems of the thinker. The longer poem *La Fin de Satan*, in which the poet recounts Christ's last days, Peter's denial of Christ, Judas's detrayal of Christ and Barrabas's release, is more inspired. But Jesus's efforts seem to have been futile. The world is still awaiting its savior. Some critics of Hugo's works go as far as to imply that Hugo assumed, himself, the task of completing the unfinished work of the Savior. But they are attributing more unconscious arrogance to Hugo than he really had. For many of the poet's notes show him to be a thinker who can be humble and confess that he does not know very much in many cases. But be that as it may, the fact remains that evil has not disappeared from the world. Nimrod, Torquemada, and other symbols of evil carry on with their machinations.

When will it be possible to say: Men, evil exists no more? . . .
Oh, Night! What emerged from Jesus was Caiaphas.

Hugo declares that the flogging of Christ goes on. Righteous men are still condemned, saints are martyrized, and prophets are slaughtered. The church is the diabolical element of religion, with its narrow-minded dogmas, especially concerning the everlasting nature of punishment, in the eyes of the poet, who shared the same outlook in this respect as his contemporaries Dostoevski and Renan. Christ was "the Supreme Man," "an immense dawn," but there is still a yawning chasm at Golgotha "where sinister religion killed God." The Supreme Sage who will finally dispel the darkness is yet to come. This Sun that will shine after the dawn will eradicate superstitions, reject narrow-minded dogmas such as the Trinity (which Hugo discarded), and will abolish Hell. The true law of love and forgiveness will then reign supreme. "Forgiveness is greater than Cain and includes him," said Hugo in "Le Griffon" in the poem *Dieu,* and yet Cain was the perfect symbol of heinous crime for Hugo. Christ had not gone far enough, but as Hugo wrote to Michelet, who had considered Christ too gentle to be crucified, Christ was a great reformer and precursor. Hugo declared to Michelet that Voltaire's cry, "Let us crush the Beast!," could have been uttered by Christ. But before that, he said shrewdly and humorously, "I rescue Jesus Christ from priests, I take the martyr down from the crucifix, and I unhook him from Christianity."

EIGHT

EVIL

Hugo seemed to be more preoccupied by God's plans for the universe and by the ever-recurring enigma of the presence of evil in the world. Even table turning threw little light on this. When the poet asked the tables: "Can you define God?" the answer, marvelously typical of Hugo and abstruse in its high-mindedness, was: "An infinite look into eternal sorrow." However, Hugo expressed himself more clearly in "Ce que dit la Bouche d'Ombre" and some notes written at the same time that he wrote *William Shakespeare*, the book that is the key to his philosophy. God, the creator of all things, had to make creation imperfect. This was not because he did not have total power but because creation would have become one with the creator and been lost in him if it had been identical with him. Creation is separation of a part of God from himself; therefore, it is necessarily imperfect. So in each being there is a small fragment of the Divine that has designed it, but in each there is also "matter." This matter is evil; it is mass that took shape and fell. Here Hugo seems to have summarized and idealized a few concepts he might have picked up, through books or conversations, in ancient esoteric tradition and particularly in the Cabala. But the poetic and picturesque form in which he presents these very vague hypotheses gets them across to his reader. This is the case in his magnificent development on the shadow that is always with us and that results

From this body, which, created by your original sin,
Having rejected God, resists light;
From your material aspect; alas! from your iniquity.

Our material aspect will be destroyed when we die, but our souls will be restored to God after a more or less long period of waiting and sometimes after transmigrations into the bodies of nonhuman beings. But this evil was necessary, for it contained a source of good. Without evil and without doubt, which is equally necessary and beneficial in its effects, man would never have created anything. He would not have been free to choose to wander and get lost, but neither would he have been free to choose good and to repent and pray, if necessary.

As a free man, he knows where good ends and evil begins;
He is judged by his actions.

This is what Hugo declared, or rather what he learned from the spirit. These views strangely resemble those expressed shortly after by the author of *The Brothers Karamazov*. Even suffering is justified. Unlike certain Russians, Hugo certainly does not make a religion of suffering, but as he said in *Les Misérables,* it can help to "expand the soul" and make it glimpse the dawn in the darkest hours of the night. Instead of rising up the ladder of creation, the soul can go down it and fall right down to the level of animals or rocks. But Hugo was always convinced that the trials of the soul could not go on forever. Its redemption comes through love; for according to Hugo, who is a greater poet of love than is generally believed, for both bodies and purified spirits, to love is "to take part in the most intimate aspects of creation." After magnificent series of alexandrines, which set forth moral law and declare the importance of duty, which man cannot escape, Hugo ends the six hundred lines dealing with the revelation made by Rozel's spirit with a hymn in six-line stanzas. The reign of love and good will come; as in the *novus ordo saeclorum* of Vergil and the

Greeks, animals will all be as gentle as lambs, monsters will be submissive, and fear, hatred, prisons, and abysses will have van-ished.

> Keep hoping, you wretched souls!
> There is no everlasting sorrow, no incurable ill,
> No eternal hell!

Man will no longer commit the crime of despising animals and torturing his more lowly brothers, a crime considered particularly heinous by Hugo, who expressed his pity for the maltreated toad. Like the priest Jocelyn, who granted immortality to his dog when he returned to his rural parish residence, Hugo calmly declared:

> Through the jungle of immense nature,
> Scenting eternity with its misshapen snout,
> There, in the shadows, at your feet, man, your dog sees God.

(In the long poem entitled *Dieu,* in the section "L'Ange," Hugo came back to this point, which he considered of capital importance: "Oh, disdain for animals and contempt for things! Man's twin faults and his twin misfortunes!")

NINE

SATAN AND HELL

Between about 1850 and 1860, at the time when Hugo relentlessly worked hardest at investing his philosophical ideas
with a poetic form, a wave of pessimism swept over Western
Europe and even sapped the extraordinary vitality of the exile.
No doubt this despair was felt less intensely by Hugo than it was
by Heine, Wagner, Baudelaire, Leconte de Lisle, Flaubert,
Matthew Arnold, and James Thomson, or by materialistic and
scientistic philosophers. Hugo could evoke the blind destruction
that broke loose in nature (volcanoes, hurricanes, worlds dying,
and the earth sobbing loudly) and proclaim, with more tragic
emotion, the implacable law whereby all things on land and in
water destroy each other. There is an eloquent development of
this theme in *Les Travailleurs de la Mer* (II, IV, 2), and Hugo has
written many macabre poems about worms that devour the bones
of dead bodies and roses that feed on our blood. One only has to
compare the great funeral ode to Théophile Gautier in *Toute la
Lyre* with other more somber poems published in the anthology
Le Tombeau de Théophile Gautier in 1872, with Mallarmé's "Toast
funèbre," for example, and especially with Leconte de Lisle's
nihilistic sonnet "A un poète mort," to admire Hugo's more
courageous and, no doubt, more philosophical attitude. Even in
the sixth book of *Les Contemplations,* in the very midst of melancholy utterances on the dune and the awfulness of the decomposition of bodies, Hugo rose to his greatest heights in more joyful

poems such as "Eclaircie." Elsewhere, Hugo attacked most relentlessly the evil done by men to their fellow beings, the injustice, hunger, poverty, prostitution, and child labor imposed on
them. To mitigate this evil seemed more philosophical to him
than speculating about its origin, in the wake of so many others.

This evil is symbolized by Satan, and, among the many por-
trayals of the Prince of Darkness in nineteenth-century French
literature, in the works of Vigny, Balzac, and Baudelaire, for
example, Hugo's is the most striking. Hugo was far from being
satanic, for he never identified himself with the Devil, as
Baudelaire did, nor did he consider making a compact with him.
To him, Satan is the perfect symbol of the exile. Claudel, who
was hard on Hugo but who, nevertheless, had much in common
with him, clearly saw and indicated that this "outlaw," this exile
who is cast down into the abysses, but who is going to ascend the
heights and earn the right to light and forgiveness, is Hugo's true
hero. *La Fin de Satan* is one of the two great philosophical epics
ever written in French, the other being *Dieu*.

The Tempter, the Evil One, whose crimes are not revealed to
us, has been swallowed up by the darkness for thousands of years.
God has condemned him, and Satan defies the judge who defeated him. Hell will be his domain, for he is denied admittance
in heaven. The light dims, and evil and darkness invade the
abyss into which Satan falls. This fallen angel sprouts wings,
which are those of "the bat in the eternal dungeon." However, a
feather that blows off the wings of the condemned angel remains
caught near Heaven. God decides that it should not be thrown
into the abyss along with Satan: "Do not throw down what has
not fallen."

After this prologue, one of the high points of Hugo's imagination, the spectacle of evil, for which Satan is responsible by
remote control, and of which he is the accursed tool, is unveiled
before the eyes of the poet and of the reader. There is an evocation of Isis-Lilith, "The demon's daughter, whom Man slept with
/ Before Eve appeared on earth," the gall that Adam tasted before

honey, whose other names are Fate, Fortune, and Ananke. Flood
and chaos have taken over. They have not, however, been able
to destroy bronze, wood, and stone, and the symbols of pervading
evil will be fashioned out of these materials: the bronze sword
representing war, along with a monumental picture of Nimrod,
who symbolizes war; the gallows, an atrocious instrument in
wood, symbolizing the crime of mankind, who crucified their
Redeemer at Golgotha; and finally, prison, more particularly the
Bastille, made out of stone, for political tyranny was not suppres-
sed by Jesus Christ and his church has even had a hand in it.

But the feather that escaped the tremendous disaster remains
on the brink of the abyss. A ray from God's eyes falls upon it, and
it quivers, grows in size, and stands erect, proud, and pure. It
becomes an angel and is called Liberty. Satan, writhing in agony
and derisive at first, groans in his exile. He loves God and pro-
claims it. His laments become moving.

> Hell is eternal absence,
> Hell is loving. Hell is saying: Alas! Where is my light?
> Where is my life and its radiance?

Satan had felt he would always be able to loathe God; but he
finds that he loves him, and that is the cause of his suffering. "If I
did not love him, I would not suffer," he exclaims. He asks for
pardon and mercy. He, too, is craving for love. He will finally be
forgiven. "No, I do not hate you," says God at the end of the
poem. Satan has understood God's secret and his supreme pity,
which makes him save the world, which is a prey to evil, through
his intervention. God's secret is love. The Evil One, on the
point of being pardoned, declares at the end of the poem:

> Oh! The essence of God is love. And man believes
> That God is but a soul like him, and that he stays aloof
> From the universe, that tremendous dust which flies away. . . .

But God responds to cries of distress. The angel Liberty is the
link between Satan and him:

She is both your daughter and mine;
This sublime paternity unites us.

God had put man in bondage, but Liberty freed him; and thanks to her, Satan, too, is saved and is reborn as the celestial Lucifer, once again a bearer of light.

No doubt there may be a certain resemblance between some of Hugo's scenes of the fall and the final pardon of Satan and some parts of the Cabala and the Zohar, although the similarities outlined by Denis Saurat may very well be explained by the fact that the authors had a similar type of imagination. This would certainly not be the first case of polygenesis in literature or in science. Perhaps Alexandre Weill expressed views of this kind when talking with Hugo; but his works were written after 1854–55, the period during which Hugo, inspired by the spiritualistic séances, composed these many long series of lines. *La Fin de Satan*, which was never completed, was published only in 1886. But as early as March 8, 1855, when Jesus Christ, through the medium of the tables, had indicated his desire for a new gospel, Hugo had joyfully replied: "I am writing a poem entitled *Satan pardoned.*" Rigorous thinkers, well versed in philosophical matters, have hailed this poem (and *Dieu,* which is a perfect complement to it, and is almost equally beautiful) as "one of the masterpieces of human mythology." Renouvier was one of the first to declare that, in this book on "metamorphosis," which takes place against a backdrop of Judeo-Christian legends, we come face to face with "a philosophy which is as profound as any ever conceived by any great philosopher." A critic who is not given to exaggeration, thanks to his linguistic training and outstanding clear-sightedness, Michael Riffaterre, declared more recently: "In French literature, *Dieu* is perhaps the philosophical poem in which poetry and philosophy are best integrated." In all the literatures of modern Europe, only Milton's *Paradise Lost* has risen to such heights and has created such myths.

TEN

THE SOCIAL PHILOSOPHY OF PROGRESS

The word *myth* often reappears in recent criticism of Hugo's work and is even found in the titles of works by Pierre Albouy, Albert Py, René Journet, and Guy Robert. There is the myth of the people, the myth of democracy, the myth of the Revolution and more particularly of the Bastille taken by storm, and finally the myth of progress. In as limited a framework as that of this work, it is impossible to deal with Hugo's political attitude or philosophy. Ambitious plans and frustrated hopes no doubt played some part in the former peer's political evolution between 1848 and 1851. However, sentiment played the largest part in this. This sentiment led the poet more and more to reject atheism—which he, like Robespierre, would almost have considered aristocratic—just as he rejected royalism, which he declared incompatible with God. "The divine excludes the royal. . . . There is no king because there is a God. Every monarchy is a usurpation of the powers of Providence." These strange statements are found in the "Philosophical Preface" to *Les Misérables,* which Hugo cut out of the completed novel. Too verbal to be a mystic and aspire to silence, Hugo was, on the other hand, too much in the public eye not to become, after his exile, the eulogizer of democracy and of the Revolution. "The Revolution and the Republic are indivisible," he proclaimed to the Legislative Assembly as early as July 1851. Like Michelet—although Michelet had reservations about some aspects of the Revolution, which he did not accept in toto—Hugo saw in this French Revolution a noble action on God's part, and therefore he considered the soldiers of the Revolution as priests. He was convinced that the spread of democracy would bring about universal peace. If he was mistaken, his erroneous ideas or chimerical hopes were shared by many far more systematic thinkers.

During the years when it was fashionable to disparage Hugo's philosophy and to refer to his love of the people with a condescending smile, some critics tried to impute a demagogic intent to his eulogies of democracy and the Republic. Actually, the pride that Hugo felt, as of 1851, in belonging to the country that had brought about the Revolution, was inspired in him by a very rational philosophy of history as well as by a noble hope. When he was in exile, Hugo made the following fervent declaration in that bizarre and rambling work *William Shakespeare* (Book II: "Le XIXe siècle"):

> The Revolution is France purified. One day, France happened to be set ablaze. Fire makes certain stubborn martyrs grow wings, and from the flames this martyred country emerged as an archangel. Today throughout the universe, France is called Revolution; and henceforth the word Revolution will be the name of civilization until it is replaced by the word Harmony. It cannot be repeated too often that the origins of nineteenth-century literature can only be found in the Revolution. . . .

In this same work, Victor Hugo, who had confessed elsewhere to having been a socialist at heart long before becoming a republican, proposed a moral goal for socialism, that of improving the lot of the masses by education and "transforming the common herd into a people." The following text, which few people will look for in this confusing book, deserves to be cited here:

> Transforming the common herd into a nation is a mammoth task to which the men who are called socialists have dedicated themselves for the last forty years. The author of this book, however

slightly socialist he may be, is one of the earliest ones. *Le Dernier Jour d'un Condamné* goes back to 1828, and *Claude Gueux* to 1834. If he claims a place for himself among these philosophers, it is because he is ready to be persecuted. A certain, very blind, but very general hatred of socialism has been rampant for the last fifteen or sixteen years, and it is still rife and keeps bursting forth among the influential classes, for classes are still with us. It must not be forgotten that the aim of true socialism is to raise the masses to civic dignity, and that, consequently, its main concern is to prepare them morally and intellectually. The most urgent need is for knowledge; so, socialism wants, above all, to educate the masses. And yet, socialism is slandered and socialists are denounced. . . . (*William Shakespeare*, V: "Les esprits, et les masses," II)

Hugo was not so naïve as to fail to recognize the tremendous excesses committed by Camille Desmoulins and, even more so, by the guillotiners in Paris, the extremists in Lyons, and those who participated in the noyades in Nantes. However, as he said in a line found in *Toute la Lyre:* "Good sometimes sprouts amidst the thorns of evil." Those who are forward-looking can at least hope to draw a useful lesson from these moments of madness and look to the future with confidence. A beautiful sentence in *Post-Scriptum de ma vie* contains possibly the finest definition ever given of political action. "The secret of great government is to know exactly how much of the future can be introduced into the present."

However, Hugo never theorized systematically or deeply on the various forms of government or the legislative means to make the most humble citizen a party to government decisions. He was less interested in political issues than he was in social problems and society's obligation to alleviate poverty, which it has tolerated, if not encouraged, for too long. The poem from *Les Châtiments* that is partially cited in the second section of this work, and that was inspired by the poet's visit to Lille, and later the poem "Les Malheureux" in *Les Contemplations*, which is one of the high points of Hugo's work, as well as other at times more facile poems such as "Les Pauvres Gens," have greatly contributed to developing a spirit of social fraternity and mutual aid in the twentieth century among those who had learned these reams of poetry by heart. Les Misérables, which it was the fashion for a while to deride but which, since 1940, has been considered by experts to be one of the very great novels of the last century, has had a profound influence on French and non-French alike, an influence such as perhaps no other novel has ever had. It contains philosophy in action that is just as good as the speculation of theorists. In a work on social history, which is strongly backed up by facts and statistics, Classes laborieuses et Classes dangereuses à Paris pendant la première moitié du dix-neuvième siècle (Plon, 1958), Louis Chevalier, a historian of nineteenth-century Paris, came to the conclusion that the problems concerning the poverty and alienation of the proletariat, caused by the industrial revolution, had been best understood not by the politicians, sociologists, and economists of the time, but by the author of the novel Les Misérables. Sentiment, too, can inspire clearsightedness and philosophical insight. In his Post-scriptum de ma vie, Hugo had boldly stated the two pillars of his faith:

> I will resist skeptical doubt, no matter where it comes from, and no one will take away from me either my love for the common man or my faith in God.

Hugo's philosophy culminates logically and chronologically (especially as of 1860) in a great profession of faith in the future of mankind. Here again, critics have derided the ingenuousness of the idealistic poet, sometimes given to prophetic declamation. The years during which he expressed his hope in the future of man were precisely those between 1850 and 1875, after the failure of several revolutions in Europe in 1848 and after the massacres and fires of the Commune, at a time when pessimism had pervaded the philosophy, poetry, novel, and arts of Western

Europe. Belief in progress, which had been passed on from Tur-
got and Condorcet to the disciples of Saint-Simon and Fourier, to
Lamartine and George Sand, seemed dead. Leconte de Lisle, the
poet who had come to France from the island of La Réunion and
who had been disillusioned by the failure of the Revolution of
1848, said in his *Dies irae:* "Universal evil is at its peak."
Baudelaire and many others condemned the myth of progress,
which negated original sin for which there is no redemption
except by divine grace, as the worst of modern heresies. The
burden of one's heredity, which Zola later dwelt on, the development of mechanization, the materialism of the masses, and
the bondage of the senses tethering man who senselessly aspired
to being an angel—these were themes of the literature written
between about 1850 and 1875, and they totally belied the dreams
of those who would have liked to believe in the betterment of
man. Nevertheless, Hugo dared, both in verse and in prose, to
reassure those of his contemporaries who were inclined to get
discouraged about the future. But he was the only one to do so,
with the exception of Walt Whitman, across the ocean.

"Do not be afraid of the march of progress," whispers a voice
in *Dieu.* This progress is brought about by science, and the flight
of lyricism in "Plein Ciel," at the end of *La Légende des Siècles,* is
one of the most daring and sustained in the literary beauty of its
stanzas in the poetry of the last century. Progress often comes
about through suffering, through personal and collective ordeals,
and even through wars and revolutions. The image of Enjolras
standing on the barricade, describing the horizon he sees in the
distance and the happy future awaiting man, compares favorably
with the most magnificent of the epics of antiquity. Finally and
above all, the betterment of man's fate will result from more
love. In novels such as *Les Misérables* and *L'Homme qui rit,* which
certainly take into account the great depths of depravity and
villainy to which man can sink, and in little-read poetic works
such as *La Pitié suprême, L'Ane,* and *Religions et Religion* could
easily be found splendid passages to make up an anthology deal-

EXCERPTS FROM
HUGO'S WRITINGS

GOD, THE ABSOLUTE, PRAYER, RELIGIONS

THE DIARY OF EXILE

God does exist. But as he is absolute and perfect, he has not created the absolute and the perfect, for otherwise he would have reproduced his own image. Thus God created the imperfect and relative, and within this creation he placed man. Man suffers because he is in an imperfect and relative environment. He suffers because he expiates in this life a sin committed in a previous life. He does not really know what this original sin is, but he is certainly aware of it. This consciousness of original sin is an integral part of every religion.

Man can return to his original, happy existence if his behavior justifies it. Similar changes can occur in nature. Mineral life becomes organic, plant life, which, in its turn, becomes animal life, the most superior species of which is the monkey. Intellectual life begins above the level of the monkey. Man is on the lowest rung of the ladder of intellectual life, an invisible and immense ladder leading to eternity and God.

(Hugo's remarks recorded by Adèle Hugo in
Journal de l'exil, April 17, 1852)

In this century, I am the first person to have spoken not only about the soul of animals but also about the soul of things. Whenever I have seen a branch of a tree being broken or a leaf being pulled off, I have said: "Leave the branch alone; leave the leaf alone. Do not disturb the harmony of nature. . . ."

When I say "the soul of inorganic matter," I believe that the soul, hemmed in and hidden, is completely passive. When I say "the soul of animals," I still believe that the soul, although less hemmed in and hidden than in inorganic matter, is nevertheless three-quarters passive and only lets instinct through. Thus, the soul of an animal plays a part in the actions of an animal but in a rather ambiguous way. . . .

The lot of animals is far worse than ours. Their soul is in the same

ing with the reasons man has to have faith in the future despite
all the regression that his fragile civilization has gone through in
the last century. Baudelaire scoffed privately at certain ingenuous
remarks in Les Misérables, which would, indeed, seem amusing to
a dandy. But both in his 1862 article and in the review published
the preceding year in La Revue fantaisiste he publicly paid tribute
to the poetic and philosophical imagination of the older poet.
No other contemporary of Hugo's has sung his praises in such a
clear-sighted manner:

> Right from the beginning, Victor Hugo was the most gifted man,
> the most obvious choice to express through poetry what I will call
> the mystery of life. (Réflexions sur quelques-uns de mes contempo-
> rains, 1861)

> Victor Hugo is for Man, and yet he is not against God. He has
> faith in God, and yet he is not against Man. . . . He believes that
> Man is born good, and yet, even when faced with his constant
> calamities, he does not accuse God of being cruel and malicious.
> (Article on Les Misérables, 1862)

terrible situation in which Paganini would be, were he locked up in a tower, blind and deaf, with nothing but a baton. However much of a genius he may be, he would inevitably remain unknown.

(Hugo's remarks recorded by Adèle Hugo in
Journal de l'exil, September 1854)

SCIENCE AND THE ABSOLUTE

Synthesis, say the heavens. Analysis, says man.

You say: "Everything is a vegetable or a mineral.
Our forefathers were led astray by their dreams."—
You think you can find the answers by tearing things apart.
The thunderbolt that caused the magus and the druid to tremble
Now is for you scientists only a fluid
Which has to be vitreous if it is not resinous.
For you, the soul is a gas, which certain animals have within them.
Men, you dissect miracles and turn
The dreams of prophets into subjects of chemistry;
You consecrate the melting-pot *principium et fons;*
Relentlessly, you cut up profound prodigies,
Prodigies that are elusive, secret, intact and unalterable,
Into intangible little pieces piled together.
For you, the present is the only reality.
Science, your scalpel learns only through destruction.
If your name were not science, it could well have been envy.
You, the living, reduce the august cloak of life—nature—
To rags and tatters, to nothingness;
And while the worms in graves call that eating,
You call that learning.
Oh knowledge! All you can do is decompose the being!
Since knowledge is your god, know this then:
Fluids, carried along by an invisible breath,
Do not know where the poles of a battery are.
The pupil does not know a thing about optics,
Nor figures about algebra, nor elements about science.

The being is a magnet attracting everything without knowing the
    forms;
All forces are enormous blind things.

The absolute is unchanging and complete.
The absolute is not aware of your pedestal, you dwarfs,
Nor of your visions, you larvae, nor of your sounds, you puppets.
It is oblivious of your swarming eyes and minds and glasses,
Of the flow and ebb of human endeavors.
It does not know if light takes five minutes
To travel thirty-five million leagues through the blue depths,
From the sun, the fire of the infinite,
To the earth, that frightful globe, impure, diseased, and exiled,
Rolling around in the host of shadows down below;
Or whether the snail takes fifteen days or sixteen hours
To do just a mile.
The sundial, the shadow of which is reflected in the deep recesses of
    your palaces;
The timepiece, ticking away your days,
Swaying dumbly in a void;
The hands of the clock, plodding dumbly around the arena,
Drawing out the hour from the well of eternity
And dashing it noisily on your frail heads;
Your flashes, your slowness, your brazen as well as claylike substance;
The rhythm of your voices and the tempo of your steps;
Your spacing and your timing—these are all unknown to the absolute.

Does protracted pleasure finally writhe in suffering?
Did Shakespeare's name take one hundred and fifty years
To cross the channel and reach France?
Is the equator torrid and the pole glacial?
Did someone called Alizuber, a lieutenant of the Prophet,
Jousting in battles as if they were solemn festivals,
Ever emerge from a combat, covered in blood and dust and smoke,
Without collecting in the evening the dust from his dark attire
In order to place it in his grave?
Is Crédit Foncier better than Grand'Combe?
Did Louis, called the Great, succeed in Flanders
Thanks to the counsel of Harcourt and Torcy?

Did Tiberius Caesar float along in his galley and dream?
And did the wind, that demagogue, have something to say about that?
Was Paul an orthodox and Philip an Arian?
The absolute sees and knows nothing of all this.
The absolute does not know who I am, nor who you are.
It alone, which is neither good nor bad, which planes over us,
Which leaves us absolutely free to say as much or as little as we please,
Has the awesome impartiality of being everything:
It has a soul; it sees the invisible;
It is the impossible; and it understands the incomprehensible.

If, in the abyss in which I am, the absolute could
Stand under the unfathomable canopy of night,
Where, according to the law of these great lairs, appear
The celestial bodies which you consider to be centres,
If the eye of providence were to fall on that,
It would be amazed at that poor little sky,
That puny firmament lit up by barely one ray,
That trickle of light that you call the dawn,
That sun, blinking through a dark fog,
The slight splendor of which spreads through the sky
Without even causing an eagle to blink,
That shadow, and the snail's pace of light.

(Toute la Lyre, III, 56)

OH! PHILOSOPHY IS INSATIABLE

Oh! Philosophy is insatiable! It takes in
Both ideas and facts, objects and words,
The known and the unknown, the real and the impossible.
It cannot progress without all this nourishment;
It is only by making full use of everything that this unwieldy cachalot
Manages to swim, to cruise along, to navigate and to stay afloat.

Look! The journey has begun. The ship glides along the shore.
All Greece seems like a world of dreams.
The throbbing vessel, which makes its way through the blue waters,
Its lungs black with coal and its breath full of fire,

Drifts past headlands, islets and inlets.
It moves ever forward. The passengers, speaking many tongues,
Stand together on the deck of the steamer and gaze
In the morning at some tranquil port, and in the evening at the sea
Turned dark red by the setting sun,
At the archipelago where the water crashes against the many reefs,
At the conical summit of the extinct volcano at Lemnos,
At Crete, and the mountains which rise like battlements,
At Corinth and Mycenae and Nauplia,
At the ruins of the Erechtheum, and the tower of Cyrrhestes,
And, far in the distance, Mount Othrys and Mount Cnemis,
Those somber giants slumbering in the Homeric night.
The paddle-steamer moves on, rapidly propelled,
Through the iridescent waves and the opaline coast,
And vast horizons stretch out alongside,
Streaked with pink clouds and sulfurous rays;
Island follows island, some lurking from view, some dawning in the
    distance.
And throughout the journey, the vessel devours
Tons of coal from Newcastle and from Cardiff.

Thus the human mind, greedy although slow,
In its journey around systems, consumes
Eternity, time, death, life and man.
And it does all that only to fail to reach the ultimate goal.

It sails on without a pilot and without a compass;
It dreams of an accessible shore in every distant land;
It tries to penetrate the impenetrable and fathom the unfathomable;
This is the work of the human mind when it seeks to unveil the
    heavens.
Philosophy drifts along in the gloomy abyss of eternity.
How can God be reached? It does not know the paths.
And often, in its meandering through the dark spaces,
It jettisons its cargo, good and bad, false and true,
Only to flounder on the impassable reef called Nothing,
That obscure rock where, constantly dashed by waves of doubt,
The great Spinoza, run aground in the darkness, rails on.

                                              (*Toute la Lyre*, III, 10)

CHEF-D'OEUVRE

You attribute the following reasoning to the good Lord:

—Formerly, in a charming, well-chosen spot,
I placed the first woman with the first man;
They ate an apple in spite of my forbidding it.
This is why I must punish man for evermore.
I make them miserable on earth, and in the fires of hell
Where Satan rakes the embers
I pledge them continual punishment for a sin which is not theirs.
Their souls go up in flames and their bodies are burned to a cinder.
Nothing is more just. But, as I am very kind,
It grieves me to do this. Alas! What should I do? Oh! I have an idea!
I will send my son to Judea, and men will kill him.
Thus—and this is why I agree to this—
Having committed a crime, they shall be innocent.
Seeing them thus commit a real crime,
I will forgive them those they have not committed;
They were virtuous, but I will turn them into criminals;
Thus I can clasp them in my arms like a father.
Thus the human race can be saved,
With its innocence washed away by a crime.

(*Religions et Religion*)

THE GREAT ONE

The great One, the great Whole, the being which Thales tried to
    penetrate
Interconnects the world of the spirit with that of objects,
And links and unifies with his inflexible laws
Moral orbits and observable ones.
Both on the ethereal level and on the real level,
Phenomena, both dark and bright, are bound together.
There is only one weaver, and he weaves only one piece of cloth.
The truth is no less a heavenly being than a star;
The sun is no more a focal point than a virtue.

So imagine, windswept dreamer,
Ensembles of moral questions, portentous problems,
Which have their justification and have it within themselves,
In a system similar to the course of the planets,
Revolving around God as planets do around the sun.
(Oh, dreamer! I say God, but I could say the Centre.)
They move to and fro; while one moves away, another moves in, and
    yet another returns,
And they pass one another like ghosts.
A certain fact which is the basis of your convictions
And which brings out the scientist and sage in you
Is often nothing but outward appearance, a phantasm, a fleeting
    element.
Man, do you know of the revolution
Of idea and passion and their interplay?

Do you know the real and the possible?
Are all functions clearly visible to you?
Sad passerby in the vale of shadows,
Do you know everything that turns around the unknown axis,
And the whole of the planetary system?
As, in tracing its orb, your mystery
Comes close in the inevitable circle
To the other vague mystery that you call evil,
Should you not account for this coincidence?
The more or less difficult flight in the more or less dense air,
The eagle that is made for the heavens and the spirit that is made for
    love,
Such harmony will become clear to you one day.

The real is pregnant with the ideal;
What is hidden from your view is open to ours;
What is visible to you is invisible to us;
There is an abstract, terrible and, at the same time, pleasant world,
Which you are unaware of but which is linked to your own,
Like one tree to another by branches intertwined;
The universe binds together, in an eternal order,
Both the moral and the carnal cogs of the wheels of life;

Actual occurrences which bring on tears, joy and rage
Correspond to other realities in thought and mind;
On the single axis on which the whole being is constructed,
Along with the dazzling zodiac of the night,
Turns the frightening zodiac of mystery;
The darkness seems to fall silent, even as it speaks;
All these facts can be perceived by you
When your eyes, opened by death, can see,
As you now see the sky sparkling with stars,
The vast constellation of souls.

(*Toute la Lyre*, III, 23)

PRAYER

Hence it is that, in the preceding book, I spoke of a convent with
respect. The Middle Ages aside, Asia aside, and the historical and
political question reserved, in the purely philosophical point of view,
beyond the necessities of militant polemics, on condition that the
monastery be absolutely voluntary and contain none but willing de-
votees, I should always look upon the monastic community with a
certain serious, and, in some respects, deferential attention. Where
community exists, there likewise exists the true body politic, and where
the latter is, there too is justice. The monastery is the product of the
formula: "Equality, Fraternity." Oh! how great is liberty! And how
glorious the transfiguration! Liberty suffices to transform the monastery
into a republic!

Let us proceed.

These men or women who live within those four walls, and dress in
haircloth, are equal in condition and call each other brother and sister.
It is well, but do they do aught else?

Yes.

What?

They gaze into the gloom, they kneel, and they join their hands.

What does that mean?

V

Prayer

They pray.

To whom?

To God.

Pray to God, what is meant by that?

Is there an infinite outside of us? Is this infinite, one, inherent, permanent; necessarily substantial, because it is infinite, and because, if matter were wanting to it, it would in that respect be limited; necessarily intelligent, because it is infinite, and because, if it lacked intelligence, it would be to that extent, finite? Does this infinite awaken in us the idea of essence, while we are able to attribute to ourselves the idea of existence only? In other words, is it not the absolute of which we are the relative?

At the same time, while there is an infinite outside of us, is there not an infinite within us? These two infinites (fearful plural!) do they not rest super-posed on one another? Does not the second infinite underlie the first, so to speak? Is it not the mirror, the reflection, the echo of the first, an abyss concentric with another abyss? Is this second infinite, intelligent also? Does it think? Does it love? Does it will? If the two infinites be intelligent, each one of them has a will principle, and there is a "me" in the infinite above, as there is a "me" in the infinite below. The "me" below is the soul; the "me" above is God.

To place, by process of thought, the infinite below in contact with the infinite above, is called "prayer."

Let us not take anything away from the human mind; suppression is evil. We must reform and transform. Certain faculties of man are directed towards the Unknown; thought, meditation, prayer. The Unknown is an ocean. What is conscience? It is the compass of the Unknown. Thought, meditation, prayer, these are the great, mysterious pointings of the needle. Let us respect them. Whither tend these majestic irradiations of the soul? into the shadow, that is, towards the light.

The grandeur of democracy is that it denies nothing and renounces nothing of humanity. Close by the rights of Man, side by side with them, at least, are the rights of the Soul.

To crush out fanaticisms and revere the Infinite, such is the law. Let us not confine ourselves to falling prostrate beneath the tree of Creation and contemplating its vast ramifications full of stars. We have a duty to perform, to cultivate the human soul, to defend mystery against miracle, to adore the incomprehensible and reject the absurd; to admit nothing that is inexplicable excepting what is necessary, to purify faith and obliterate superstition from the face of religion, to remove the vermin from the garden of God.

VI

Absolute Excellence of Prayer

As to methods of prayer, all are good, if they be but sincere. Turn your book over and be in the infinite.

There is, we are aware, a philosophy that denies the infinite. There is also a philosophy, classed pathologically, which denies the sun; this philosophy is called blindness.

To set up a sense we lack as a source of truth, is a fine piece of blind man's assurance.

And the rarity of it consists in the haughty air of superiority and compassion which is assumed towards the philosophy that sees God, by this philosophy that has to grope its way. It makes one think of a mole exclaiming: "How they excite my pity with their prate about a sun!"

There are, we know, illustrious and mighty atheists. These men, in fact, led round again towards truth by their very power, are not absolutely sure of being atheists; with them, the matter is nothing but a question of definitions, and, at all events, if they do not believe in God, being great minds, they prove God.

We hail, in them, philosophers, while, at the same time, inexorably disputing their philosophy.

But, let us proceed.

An admirable thing, too, is the facility of settling everything to one's satisfaction with words. A metaphysical school at the North, slightly impregnated with the fogs, has imagined that it effected a revolution in the human understanding by substituting for the word "Force" the word "Will."

To say, "the plant wills," instead of "the plant grows," would be indeed pregnant with meaning if you were to add, "the universe wills." Why? Because this would flow from it: the plant wills, then it has a "me"; the universe wills, then it has a God.

To us, however, who, in direct opposition to this school, reject nothing *a priori*, a will in the plant, which is accepted by this school, appears more difficult to admit than a will in the universe, which it denies.

To deny the will of the infinite, that is to say God, can be done only on condition of denying the infinite itself. We have demonstrated that.

Denial of the infinite leads directly to nihilism. Everything becomes "a conception of the mind."

With nihilism no discussion is possible. For the logical nihilist doubts the existence of his interlocutor, and is not quite sure that he exists himself.

From his point of view it is possible that he may be to himself only a "conception of his mind."

However, he does not perceive that all he has denied he admits in a mass by merely pronouncing the word "mind."

To sum up, no path is left open for thought by a philosophy that makes everything come to but one conclusion, the monosyllable "No."

To "No," there is but one reply: "Yes."

Nihilism has no scope. There is no nothing. Zero does not exist. Everything is something. Nothing is nothing.

Man lives by affirmation even more than he does by bread.

To behold and to show forth, even these will not suffice. Philosophy should be an energy; it should find its aim and its effect in the amelioration of mankind. Socrates should enter into Adam and produce Marcus Aurelius—in other words, bring forth from the man of enjoyment, the man of wisdom—and change Eden into the Lyceum. Science should be a cordial. Enjoyment! What wretched aim, and what pitiful ambition! The brute enjoys. Thought, this is the true triumph of the soul. To proffer thought to the thirst of men, to give to all, as an elixir, the idea of God, to cause conscience and science to fraternise in them, and to make them good men by this mysterious confrontation—such is the province of true philosophy. Morality is truth in full bloom. Contemplation leads to action. The absolute should be practical. The ideal must be made air and food and drink to the human mind. It is the ideal

which has the right to say: *Take of it, this is my flesh, this is my blood.*
Wisdom is a sacred communion. It is upon that condition that it ceases
to be a sterile love of science, and becomes the one and supreme
method by which to rally humanity; from philosophy it is promoted to
religion.

Philosophy should not be a mere watch-tower, built upon mystery,
from which to gaze at ease upon it, with no other result than to be a
convenience for the curious.

For ourselves, postponing the development of our thought to some
other occasion, we will only say that we do not comprehend either man
as a starting-point, or progress as the goal, without those two forces
which are the two great motors, faith and love.

Progress is the aim, the ideal is the model.

What is the ideal? It is God.

Ideal, absolute, perfection, the infinite—these are identical words.

> (*Les Misérables*, II, VII, 3–6, 1860–61.
> Translation taken from *Les Misérables*,
> translated by Charles E. Wilbour. London:
> John Lane, The Bodley Head Ltd., 1934.
> Used by permission.)

There must be those who pray constantly for those who never pray.

In our opinion, the whole question lies in the amount of thought put
into prayer. . . .

Praying is linking the infinite here below with the infinite up above
through thought.

> (*Les Misérables*, part II: "Cosette." Book VIII;
> "Parenthèse," ch. VII: "Foi, Loi")

REMARKS RECORDED BY STAPFER

I do not let four hours go by without praying. I pray regularly morning
and night. I pray again if I wake up in the dead of night. What do I pray
for?

I ask God to grant me His strength. I know what is good and what is
bad. But I am weak and I am aware of my weakness; within me alone, I
do not have the strength to do what I know is good. . . . God sustains

and protects us. We live in Him. He gives us life, movement and being. He is the Maker of everything. He is the Creator. But it is incorrect to say that He created the world. For He is constantly in the process of creating it. He is the soul of the universe. He is the Self of the infinite.

(Remarks made by Hugo in Guernsey in 1867 and recorded by Stapfer)

To the Bishop who Called me an Atheist

Athée? entendons-nous, prêtre, une fois pour toutes

Me, reverend sir, "an Atheist" you call?
Let's understand each other, once for all.
To play the spy on me, to trap my soul,
To act eaves-dropper, look through the keyhole
To the inside of my spirit, search how deep
My doubts may reach, even into hell to peep
And read the records of its dark police
Across that sea of sighs that never cease,
To see what I believe, and what deny—
Spare yourself all these needless pains, say I.
My faith is simple; here I write my creed.
I love plain words, such as who runs may read.

If we are speaking of an aged man
White-bearded, seated on a stage divan
'Twixt an archangel and a seer; a kind
Of Emperor or Pope; a cloud behind,
A bird above his head; his offspring pale
Held in his arms, pierced through with many a nail;
A jealous God, that is both one and three;
A vengeful, with an ear for psalmody;
Punishing children for their father's crime,
Hallowing royal brigands in their slime,
Stopping the sun short, every evening,
At risk of snapping off the great main-spring;
God, ignorant of science physical,
Man's counterpart in large; the same in small;

Angry at times, and somewhat given to pout,
Like Père Duchêne with his big sabre out;
Tardy in pardon, quick at condemnation,
Checking his mother's passes to salvation;
A god who, seated in his azure sky,
Makes it his business with our faults to vie,
His sport to keep a pack of miseries
As squires keep hounds; who makes disturbances;
Sets Nimrod, Cyrus loose, and gets us bitten
By Attila, and by Cambyses eaten,
I am, sir priest, whoe'er may think it odd,
An Atheist, to this good-old-fashioned God.

If, on the other hand, we have to do
With the all-essential Being above us, who
In all we are concentrates all we dream;
In whom the dissonances of nature seem
Accorded, and the universal span
Claims personality, no less than man;
That Being, whose soul I feel within my own;
Who ever pleads with me, in still small tone,
For truth against illusion, while around
The senses boil, and half my powers are drowned;
If with that witness who within has wrought
Now pain, now pleasure at a passing thought,
So that, according as I sink or soar,
The brute, or spirit, prevails in me the more;
If with that everlasting marvel, rife
With something more than we possess of life,
Wherewith our soul becomes intoxicate
As often as it comes, soaring elate,
As Jesus and as Socrates did come,
For truth, right, virtue, straight to martyrdom;
Oft as high duty impels it down the steep,
Oft as it skims a halcyon o'er the deep,
Oft as with loftier aim it penetrates
Athwart the ugly shadow of its hates,
And on the farther frontier of the gloom
Seeks for the dawn; O priest, if we assume

To speak of that First Essence, whom a creed
Neither unmakes nor makes; whom we concede
Wise, and suppose benignant; without face,
Without a body, or son; having more grace
Of fatherhood the while, and more of love,
Than summer has of sunlight from above;
If of that vast unknown, whom Holy Writ
Names not, explains not, makes not known one whit;
Of whom no scribes, no commentators speak,
Most High that looms, dim as a mountain-peak,
O'er cradled infant and enshrouded dead;
Not eatable in any unleavened bread;
If of that dizzy summit of all natures
Who speaks in tongues of elemental creatures,
(Not priests, or Bibles;) Him, who reads the abyss,
To whom the heaven of heavens a temple is;
Not sensual; not ceremonial;
The law, the life, the very soul of all;
Invisible, because He is immense;
Intangible, save that beyond our sense,
Past all those forms, which any breath can melt,
In nothing grasped, He is in all things felt;
If of the all-transcending quietude,
Solstice of reason, justice, right, and good,
Who, stable make-weight of infinity,
That is, that was, that evermore shall be,
Sets bounds to suns, gives patience in distress,
Without us light, within us consciousness;
Who hath shone ever in heaven, and under earth;
And is the Birth, and is the Second Birth;
If of the eternal, single, vast First Cause,
Whose being is His thought; whose thought, the laws
Whence all things have their being; whom I call
God, merely as the greatest name of all:
Then, we change sides. Then turn our spirits home;
Thine to the night, the mire, the ghastly gloom
Where only mockings and negations live;
Mine to the light, the august affirmative,

Hymn, ecstasy of my rapt soul! Then, Priest,
I am believer, and thou Atheist.

(*L'Année Terrible.*
Translation taken from
The Poems of Victor Hugo, vol. II.
New York: The Athenaeum Society, 1909.)

Jean Huss

Jean Huss was tied down to the stake,
Over a crackling fire.
Jean Huss saw the town executioner coming towards him,
With his monstrous, dreadful, vile face.
This was the executor of death, the infamous, atrocious, powerful,
    blood-stained slave of death,
The master of the obscure work of death,
The hideous passerby whom the worms strained to see,
The killer who kept no track of his victims and never paused,
The blind force that rotated the capstan of the law.
Everybody in town, standing at the doorstep or on the roof of a house,
Was speaking and swarming and looking on at the entertainment.
Huss saw coming towards him this man, this animal,
This wretched, inferior being haunted by terror,
This terrible creature of the night;
Deformed by the burden of eternal horror,
His pupils blazing like the flames of the faggots,
He stood there, his mouth twisting from indignity;
His forehead reflected the faces of spectres
And the sounds of countless tortures;
His whole life could be read in his melancholy face:
Isloation, mourning, anathema,
The unforgivable stigma of murder,
Death that nursed him at her breasts,
His bed made up of a section of the stake, his woman,
His children, more accursed than baby wolves,
His dismal house, where swarms of schoolboys peered through the
    chinks

Only to flee the minute he stirred;
His hands, scarred by the red-hot iron, were wrinkled;
Soldiers never mentioned his name without spitting.
He drew near the stake, that hideous caryatid,
Hunched, bent, defiled, wicked and ashamed;
He surveyed the spot where the smouldering fire was built;
He came and threw more oil and pitch on it;
He brought a load of wood over to the horrible furnace,
Perspiring and groaning because of the weight;
Before the hate-filled eyes of the people, he stirred the embers,
A despicable, wretched reprobate, blasphemed and blaspheming.
And with the ominous flames licking at him,
Jean Huss raised his eyes to heaven and murmured: Poor man!

(*La Pitié suprême,* XIV)

PHILOSOPHICAL PREFACE OF *Les Miserables*

Part One
I

The book you are about to read is a religious one.
Religious? From what point of view?
From a certain point of view that is ideal but absolute, undefined but unwavering.

• • • •

The author of this book, using his right to freedom of conscience, declares that he does not espouse any modern religion, but that, while fighting against their corrupt practices and fearing their human aspect, which is like the wrong side of their divine aspect, he accepts and respects all of them.

If ever their divine aspect eventually reabsorbed and destroyed their human aspect, he would not only respect them but also venerate them.

Having expressed these reservations, the author announces openly as he is about to begin this sad book that he believes in God and prays.

This explains his great indulgence for everything connected with religious beliefs in this work. The few religious silhouettes found in it are solemn ones. A bishop makes an appearance and casts a venerable shadow over it; a convent is glimpsed in it. The half-light which emerges is pleasing.

(Préface philosophique, *Les Misérables,* an extract)

SATAN, DEATH, THE ABYSS

Satan in the Darkness

II

Hell is eternal absence.
Hell is loving. Hell is saying: Alas! Where is my light?
Where is my life and its radiance?
Its beauty is revealed to other enraptured beholders;
It smiles up above at others; others kiss its eyes
And find joy and peace in its bosom.
Others enjoy it. I am in despair.

Oh! When I was cast down
From the heights of splendor into this state of blindness,
After darkness fell about my head,
After I, stripped naked, was hurled down for ever
From the pinnacle into the inexorable depths,
When I found myself alone at the bottom of the infinite,
I was plunged into such darkness for a moment that I began to laugh;
The vast obscurity filled me with its delirium;
In my heart, where the love of God was destroyed and dying,
I felt the strange and savage plenitude of the darkness,
And I cried out, joyous, triumphant and implacable.

"Down with the heavens filled with blinding light!
Down with the firmament, where God has introduced so many artificial
    attractions!
He thought he was driving me away, but it is I who have run away.
He thinks I am now a prisoner, but, in fact, I am free.
I feel as if I am soaring.
And the devil is the eagle, and the world the donkey.
And I laugh. I am proud and content. I have turned my back

On useless, despicable and vile angels, and on you, light,
Which corrupts them, and on you, love, which instigates them!
What joy there is in unfettered hatred!
God, the heart of the universe, the radiant father
Shared by angels, stars, men and animals,
The focal point around which the flock gathers,
The being which is the only living, true and necessary one,
I, the punished colossus, will do without.
And so it should be. How I will curse the blessed one!
And, while Adam burns incense before him, I will turn
My former power into revolt against him
And my former radiance into flame.
How I will rage at him! How I, the hideous one,
Face to face with him, the supreme being,
Will hate and loathe and abhor him!"

     I love him!—

                          (*La Fin de Satan,* III.
                          Hors de la Terre;
              I, Satan dans la nuit, II)

If I did not love him, I would not suffer thus.

Oh abysses, let me climb out of here! No. Step by step
I descend, I sink down; with every effort I make,
I slip further into the depths. The misfortune of darkness, its torment,
Is to adore light but continue to be darkness.
It is a fatal love, the consequence of which is evil.
Oh, light! Where are you? Satan is beseeching you.
Do you hear me? Return, oh dawn!
Do not tell others you will always appear. Do not tell me you will never
    appear.
I am suffering!—Oh! Everything is dark, and I see nothing.
I am filled with hatred!—Yes, I hate you, you clods, you colorless
    crowd,
Because you love God and he loves you,
Because his light shines through you,
Because you can dip your urns in the streams,

Because, as living beings, you can wander through nature,
Because, while I am racked by torture and my soul eats away at me like
  a vulture,
You have hope in your eyes and love in your hearts.

Men, larvae, shadows, faceless creatures, voids,
How come you are not happy? Oh stupid, spoiled darlings
You complain of growing older every day,
Of time passing and your aging,
And you dare to blame God! What dreams you do cherish!
I have lost more than you! I have seen my light gradually dimming,
As you have seen your hair thinning!

(*La Fin de Satan*, III.
Hors de la Terre;
I, Satan dans la nuit, IV)

Satan Forgiven

Oh! The essence of God is love. And man believes
That God is but a soul like him, and that he stays aloof
From the universe, that tremendous dust which flies away;
But I, the sad enemy and mocking, envious man,
Know that God is not a soul but a heart.
God, the loving heart of the world,
Ties all the fibres of all the roots to his own divine fibres,
And his love makes worms equal to seraphim;
And to the great astonishment of all,
This loving sun, blasphemed on earth by priests,
Has as many rays as there are beings in the universe.
For him, creating, thinking, meditating, giving life,
Sowing, destroying, making, being, and seeing is loving.
Resplendent, he loves and is adored in return.
Everything has its being in him; he is linked to darkness by dawn,
To minds by ideas, to flowers by their scent;
This heart embraces the infinite, with one exception.
This exception is Satan, eternally rejected, damned and dejected.
God excludes me; I mark the confines of his kingdom.
God would be infinite, if I did not exist.

I say to him: You did well, Lord, when you cast me out!
I certainly do not blame him. But I do despair.
Oh somber eternity, I am a fatherless son.
A fallen archangel, but no longer of God.

IV

Over and over, hundreds of times, I make my confession:
I love! While God tortures me, here is my blasphemy,
My frenzy and my howling cry: I love!
My overpowering love makes the heavens tremble!
What! Is it all in vain?
Oh! It is outrageous, horrible, and yet divine
To rise, to open wide one's foolish wings,
To cling, bleeding, to every thought
That one can seize upon, with shouts and tears,
To probe fears and to probe pains,
Those that are real and those that are imagined,
To go through the entire cycle of terror,
Only to fall again into the same despair!

> (*La Fin de Satan,* IV.
> Hors de la Terre;
> Satan pardonné, III, IV)

GOD

—Nobody is punished for the crime of another.
In any event, men, fruit is there to be picked.
The book of life is there to be read.
Knowledge is life; and life is law. Adoration
Is knowledge; and the celestial gates welcome those who wish to enter.
Whatever man's struggles and troubles and trials,
Each time that he, humble and overwhelmed by doubt,
Grasps a new fact in the darkness, he has had a taste
Of God, of light and of eternity.
And so it should be. It is one step closer to the light.
By dint of science and ceaseless endeavor,

Man rough-hews the immense statue of truth in his obscurity;
And he is right in so doing.
Man, in darkness, is the sculptor and mystery is his medium.
And this has to be. Eve was right in reaching up to the tree;
Prometheus was right and so was Galileo;
Columbus did well to find a new world at the end of the horizon.
Dante penetrated the dark depths, circle by circle;
Spinoza revealed the dreadful secrets of nothingness;
Fulton tamed the sea stirred up by Xerxes;
Galvani, followed by Volta, handled and mixed
Fluids, power, core, magnets, metals and mercury;
Mesmer, filled with awe, discovered unknown horizons.
It is your right, man, to perform such feats.
Aeschylus and Shakespeare were justified, earth, in studding your
    prison-like ceiling with stars.
Roemer stopped the delighted light in its flight;
Gutenberg created light, love and life
With the molten lead formerly used in human torture;
Pythagoras probed the shadows;
Papin harnessed to man, to the bewitched world,
To the soul and to vehicles the new black horse, the steam engine.
Halley loudly heralded the return of a comet;
Leibniz offered spiritual escape to the mind,
And, weaving together calculus, philosophy and study,
He threw into the infinite the ladder of Latude;
Harvey said: Blood flows, and man lives.
Kepler conquered the stars, and Franklin the lightning;
Jackson removed pain from the flesh that he cut into.
All these men have found truth, beauty and purpose.
Go forth! Pick up your spade and dig the garden!
Montgolfier wanted to conquer the skies while awaiting Eden;
All to the good. And Luther did well to expand the spiritual realm,
And Vesalius to throw light on that Colossus, death.
Daring is sacred and God blesses hard work.
All the blazing swords hounding Adam were wrong!
Rise, mind. God awaits you. In his two flaming hands,
For balance, he holds the celestial bodies, and, for justice, he holds
    souls;

And, as the aim of the universe is seeing and learning,
It is the duty of the heavenly bodies and of minds to shine forth. . . .

(*Dieu,* VII, L'Ange)

IN THE GRAVE

—Leave me alone.—No.—Oh, sinister claw!
Oh, yawning jaws! Oh, torture! Oh, sorrow!
Why do you slip into the darkness
Through the cracks in my coffin?

—I must derive fresh vigor,
Oh death! Here comes summer's pleasant days.
All nature that dreams,
Ghost, awaits my beauty!

No lily should hide my face;
The bees expect honey from me;
I need a scent which will delight
The swans in the sky.

I must embellish the gloomy lair;
I must smile at the sullen evening,
And bestow on everything
Some of my grace and splendor.

I must adorn
The virgin's veil at daylight;
I must breathe for the stars
And blush for love.

And while I am sprayed by the dew of dawn,
My roots reach down towards you.
Who are you?—I am a rose.
And what do you want? I am thirsting for your blood.

(*Les Quatre Vents de l'Esprit,* III, XXIII)

CONSCIENCE

Oh! quoique je sois, sur la grève

Although upon the shore I seem
A flake of foam in passing flight;
Although my life is but a dream,
Though I am only dust and night;

Though I am but a lump of clay,
A worm 'mid other human worms,
Crushed 'neath the wheel which speeds away,
The wheel which man "To-morrow" terms;

Though beneath Evil's fangs I lie;
Though I am scorned, and weak, and bare;
Though I am made of misery,
And you of heavenly azure are;—

Dauntless in right you still confide,
Immovable in trust and faith;
Conscience! my sacred help and guide,
You go before me e'en to Death!

Ever prepared, you march before;
You lead, I follow your command;
Your face, Fate's veil is gathered o'er—
The lamp of God is in your hand.

You say, "Your cross you must abide;
Rise up! Here is no resting-place."
You say, "Your soul here you must hide";
You say, "Step in the paths I trace."

You prefer life with sorrows steep,
Mourning and gloom the friend we own;
You smile when I am forced to weep,
You sing when I am forced to groan.

Lit by your torch, with rapture rife,
I, step by step, serene and brave,

Through all the miseries of life,
Pass downward to the silent grave.

(*Les Quatre Vents de l'Esprit*, III, XXXVI.
Translation taken from *The Poems of Victor Hugo*, vol. II.
New York: The Athenaeum Society, 1909.)

Night Thoughts

Here below, the most limpid darkness is that of the soul.

Man is the strange and sad enigma of woman,
And woman is the sphinx of man. Tragic fate!
Nobody knows my abyss, except me.
And have even I plumbed its depths? My abyss
Is sinister, especially by its sublime aspect;
And the Hydra hides there, clinging to my soul and gnawing at it.
All our passions are animals prowling
In the ghastliness of dim twilights.

The man most like Hercules of antiquity,
Who is equal by his stature to difficult deeds,
Who tames fortune with his unmerciful hands,
And who seems like a gladiator to jealous fate,
This man, if he meets a woman, wants to please,
Falls to his knees, adores and trembles,
And this conqueror of destiny is conquered by his heart.

Life is a constant disappointment. The hearth is not blazing, the nation
   not grateful.
Priest, think of Jesus; judge, think of Socrates.
Man renders justice just as he throws the dice.
When, turn by turn, one by one, bent over
The same book, we have turned the same pages,
We die, Where then is your Areopagus?
Where are your councils and senates, conclaves and divans?
The poet appears in the midst of the living,
And, maligned, disappears from this ill-fated earth,
Leaving behind him, like a vague trail,

The eternal beauty of mysterious verse.
Man, who insulted him, then ranks him among the gods.
Then another great mind appears, and the same cycle is repeated.
Everything is blind when it is not insane;
The radiant heavens are full of the darkness of fate;
We enter life crying; we emerge from it
Soaked through, naked and frozen, as if from a storm.
Alas! Children sob and men lament:
To be ignorant is to weep, and to have knowledge is to moan. . . .

(Les Quatre Vents de l'Esprit, III, XLII)

PILE OF STONES

If death is the end of everything for man, then what he has done in life is of little importance. The righteous and the wicked are treated in the same manner by death, which awaits them all. The distinction between crime and virtue becomes blurred and even disappears in the void of death, where inequality reigns. . . . Thus moral life, the soul, virtue, and good do not exist.

And what does the absence of good imply if not the presence of evil? Can evil be revealed in a more overwhelming and terrible way than by the fact, if it is a fact, that good does not exist?

Good does not exist; so evil does.

For what evil could be greater than the lack of good?

Is this not obvious? Just as when it is not day it is night.

So also when there is no good there is evil. . . .

In other words, evil is God.

In other words, Satan is God.

If this were not absurd, it would be appalling.

Evil is a negation . . . , a lack . . . , a No opposed to a Yes.

But what exists cannot be a negation.

For negation can only beget nothingness.

If evil were God, NOTHING WOULD EXIST.

And something does exist.

Thus evil is not God.

The infinite and eternity are necessarily affirmations.

And affirmation is the contrary of negation. So the infinite and eternity are the contrary of evil.

So the infinite and eternity constitute good.

If the infinite and eternity constitute good, good does exist.

If good exists, so does moral life, for good is its guiding light.

And moral life is nothing but the life of souls animated by God.

Thus the soul exists.

For if God exists, the soul exists. . . .

The soul is what makes man free. . . . Man is responsible (not in this life but in an after-life. A part of him survives to bear this responsibility: the soul. Death is the finale of man and the début of the soul).

(*Le Tas de Pierres,* Explication de la vie
et de la mort, August 25, 1844)

To Theophile Gautier

Friend, poet, spirit, you flee our dismal darkness.

You leave our clamorous world behind and enter the world of glory.

Henceforth your name will echo off the pinnacle of purity.

I, who knew you when you were young and handsome, I, who cared for you,

I, who, more than once, in our lofty flights,

Was bewildered and turned to you, faithful soul, for support,

I, with my hair turned white with age,

I remember bygone days, and, recalling

The period of our youth, the age of our dawn,

The struggles and storms and noisy battlegrounds,

The new art which came forth crying "Yes,"

I listen to that great sublime gust that has died away.

Son of ancient Greece and of young France,

Your proud respect for the dead was full of hope;

You never closed your eyes to the future.

You, magus at Thebes and Druid at the foot of the black menhir,

You, flamen on the banks of the Tiber and Brahman on the banks of the Ganges,

Placing in the bow of God the arrow of the archangel,
Haunting the presence of Achilles and Roland,
You, mysterious and powerful forger, you knew
How to twist all the rays into one single flame;
In your soul the setting sun became one with the dawn;
In your productive mind the past intermingled with the future;
You consecrated the old art, forefather of the new;
You understood that, when an unknown but inspired spirit,
Streaking across the heavens, has a message for the people,
You should listen to it, accept it, love and welcome it;
Calmly you scorned the vile effort of scoffers
Who raged against Aeschylus and slandered Shakespeare;
You knew that this century has its own special air,
And that, as art only develops by being transformed,
The beautiful is embellished by adding the great;
And it is well known that you exclaimed with joy
When the winter of the past was driven away by revolutionary spring,
When the unexpected star of the modern ideal
Suddenly appeared in the blazing sky,
And when the hippogriff took over from Pegasus.

I salute you on the grim threshold of death!
Go find the truth, you who knew how to find beauty.
Climb up the steep ladder. From the top of the dark steps,
From the dark bridge spanning the abyss you can glimpse the arches;
Move on! The last hour is the last step!
Take off, eagle; you will see abysses to your liking;
You will see the absolute, the real and the sublime;
You will feel the sinister wind of the summit
And be dazzled by the marvel of eternity.
You will perceive your Olympus from up in the heavens;
From the heights of truth you will see human dreams,
Including that of Job and that of Homer,
Soul, and from the level of God you will see Jehovah.
Rise, spirit! Grow, soar, take wing, go!

When a living being passes away, I gaze at him, moved;
For dying is like entering a temple;

And when a man dies, I clearly see
In his ascent my own advent.
Friend, I feel the somber plenitude of fate.
I have entered upon death through solitude;
I see the evening of my life vaguely sprinkled with stars;
It is time that I too left this world;
The thread of my life is too long, and is quivering and almost touching
   the blade;
I am being lifted by the wind which gently carried you off,
And I, the exile, will follow those who loved me.
Their glassy stare draws me to the depths of the infinite.
Thither I come. Do not close the gates of death.

Let us move on, for that is the unavoidable law;
Everything gives way, and this great century, with all its radiance,
Enters the vast darkness into which, we, with our pale faces, flee.
Oh! What a dreadful noise is being made in the twilight
By the felling of the oaks for Hercules' funeral pyre!
The horses drawing the carriage of death are neighing,
And are joyous, for the age of light is about to end.
This proud century, which succeeded in curbing the adverse wind,
Is passing away. . . . Oh, Gautier! You, who were their equal and their
   brother,
Are leaving after Dumas and Lamartine and Musset.
The ancient fountain of youth has run dry;
As there is no longer the Styx, there is no longer Youth.
The grim reaper with his large blade moves on,
Deep in thought and step by step, towards the rest of the standing corn;
Now it is my turn; darkness fills my troubled eyes,
Which, guessing, alas! the fate of doves,
Weeps over cradles and smiles before graves.

Hauteville-House, November 2, 1872, All Souls' Day.

(*Toute la Lyre*, IV, L'Art)

SOCIAL COMPASSION, MORAL LAW, REVELATION, DREAMS

THE CELLARS OF LILLE

I

Oh, looters, schemers, swindlers, cretins, powerful tyrants!
Gather quickly around the banquet of life!
Hurry! There is room for all!
Masters, drink and eat, for life is fleeting.
This conquered people, this stupid people,
This entire nation is yours!

Sell the State! Fell the trees! Steal all the money!
Empty the reservoirs and dry up the springs!
The time has come.
Take the very last cent! Steal gaily and easily
From the workers in the fields and those in the towns!
Seize, make merry and enjoy yourselves!

Go on! Feast! Live! Carouse! So it should be!
The families of the poor die in hovels,
Without a door, without even shutters.
The father, trembling, goes out to beg in the darkness;
The mother has no bread, the child no milk;
Dismal destitution!

II

Millions! Millions! Châteaux! Funds for the privileged ones!
One day I went down into the cellars of Lille;
I saw this gloomy hell.
There, underground, are phantoms in rooms,
Pale and bent over; rickets twists their limbs
In its iron grip.

Under these vaults, there is suffering; the air seems like poison;
The blindman, groping, gives a drink to the consumptive;
Water pours through the gutters;

Almost a child at twenty, but already an old man at thirty,
The poor wretch feels death penetrating, seeping
Into his bones day by day.

There is never any light; the skylight is blurred by streaming rain;
In the subterranean passages where misfortune
Dogs you, oh workers,
Near the spinning wheel which turns and the thread which unwinds,
The eye glimpses larvae wandering around in the pale glimmer
Seeping through the rain-drenched air hole.

Destitution! Men dream while gazing at women.
The father, aware that around him unspeakable distress
Shackles virtue,
Sees his daughter's ominous return,
And with his eyes fixed on the bread she is carrying,
Does not dare to say: Whence do you come?

There lies despair on its filthy rags;
There the spring of life, which, elsewhere, is warm and resplendent,
Resembles the dark winter;
The virgin, pink in the light, turns violet in the darkness;
There, in the depths of horror, crawl emaciated figures
As naked as worms.

There, buried deeper than the sewers, shiver
Families who have left behind both life and light,
Trembling groups;
There, when I entered, fierce like Medusa,
A little girl with the face of a crone
Said: I am eighteen!

There, having no bed, the poor mother
Puts her little children, trembling like birds, to sleep
In a hole she has dug;
Alas! these innocent souls with their dovelike gaze
Find at their birth a grave
Instead of a cradle!

Cellars of Lille! People are dying beneath your stone ceiling!
I have seen with my own eyes wet with tears

Withered old men in the throes of death,
Girls with haggard eyes, covered only by their hair,
And ghostlike children at the breasts of their statuelike mothers!
Oh, Dante Alighieri!

Your wealth is born of this suffering, oh Princes!
Your bounty feeds on this destitution,
Oh vanquishers! Oh conquerors!
Your riches stream down or ooze in
From the walls of these cellars, from these stony vaults,
From the hearts of these dying souls.

Under the dreadful wheels of tyranny,
Under the screws of the Treasury, that hideous genius,
From dawn to dusk,
Endlessly, night and day, in this century of ours,
Men are crushed like grapes
And gold pours out of the wine press.

From this poverty and anguish,
From this darkness, where withered hearts
Were never filled with hope,
From these dark hovels full of bitter distress,
From this dismal pack of fathers and mothers
Wringing their hands,

Yes, from this mass of hideous poverty
The great millions, sparkling, horrible,
Distributed along the way,
Moving towards power and apotheosis,
Emerge, joyous monsters, crowned with roses,
And covered with human blood.

                                    (*Les Châtiments*, IX, III)

THE UNFORTUNATE

Thus, all sufferers seemed to me splendid,
Contented, radiant, gentle, majestic, guileless,
And happy, with their wounded souls and joyful hearts;

Some, thrown into the fire, had turned into perfume,
Others, thrown into the darkness, had turned into light;
The believers, devoured in the echoing arenas,
Gasped out a song, as they lay dying beneath the animals;
The thinkers smiled at the sinister autos-da-fé,
At the swords and the iron collars and the sulphur shirts.
So I exclaimed: Who then is suffering?
If fate, oh God, is not making mock of me,
For whom is meant all this pity that you have placed in my heart?
What should I do with it? For whom should I preserve it?
Where are the unfortunate ones?—And God answered: Behold.

And I saw palaces and festivals and banquets,
And women with their white skins and satins,
And lofty walls covered with jasper,
And golden serpents wound into twisted columns,
With vast canopies hanging from the high ceilings;
And I heard the cries: Let us enjoy life! Let us triumph!
And the music of lyres and lutes and bugles whose brass
Seemed to dissolve into fanfare and to be alive,
And the organ, which makes the darkness listen and fall silent;
An entire orchestra, large and monstrous, was playing;
And this triumph was filled with magnificent men
Who laughed and carried the whole earth in sheaves,
And whose golden, shining, daring and proud
Foreheads seemed to end up as stars in the heavens.
And while around them voices cried:—Victory
For ever! Strength, power and glory for ever!
Gaiety in the town and joy in the home!—
I saw hanging above the pale horizon
The huge black sword of the archangel.

They bloomed in a strange dawn,
They lived in pride, as if it were their realm,
And seemed to be aware only of their felicity.
And God took them all, one after the other,
The powerful, the sated, and the satiated,
The Czar from his Kremlin, and the imam from the banks of the Nile,

Like puppies taken from a kennel,
And, as he brings light to the depths of the sea,
He opened up with his hands these deep chests,
And probed with his finger of light
Their entrails, their livers and their loins,
And showed me the serpents that were gnawing at their innards.

And I saw these men and women shudder with fear;
Their laughing faces fell away like a mask,
And their thoughts, frightful, deformed monsters,
Wild, anxious, churlish dwarfs,
Hidden under their dreadful skulls, were revealed to me.
Then, trembling and quaking,
I asked them: "Who are you?"
And these almost faceless beings
Answered: "We are those who do evil; and, as
It is we who do evil, it is we who have to endure it."

Oh! The useless downpour of tears and affronts
Ceases, and suffering vanishes, crying: Hope!
You made me see and feel this, oh Father,
Oh Judge, you, the just one, you, the merciful one!
The laughter of success and triumph is deceptive;
An invisible hand caresses each of those
Linked in human misery;
Adversity sustains those that it forces to struggle;
Poverty is an asset for those who know how to appreciate it;
Eternal harmony embraces the poor
And cradles them; the slave, being a soul, is free,
And the beggar says: I am rich, having God.
The innocent in anguish cry: It could be worse.
Aesop laughs despite his deformity and Scarron
Despite his fever; the dying sing hymns of praise;
When I ask: "Is pain an evil?" Zeno
Appears before me and calmly answers: "No."
Oh! Martyrdom is joy and rapture; corporeal punishment
Is sensual gratification; burning at the stake is delight;

Suffering is pleasure; torture is happiness;
The only unfortunate beings are the wicked, Lord.

In the early days of the world, when the clouds,
Surprised, gazed at everything created,
When over the earth, where evil had germinated,
A gleam from Paradise Lost still hovered,
When all still seemed full of the light of dawn,
When the years had just blossomed on the tree of time,
On earth, where flesh and spirit blended,
In the evening there was a great silence,
And the desert, the woods, the sea with its vast shores,
And the grass in the fields, and the wild animals,
All moved, and the rocks, those dark dungeons,
Saw emerging from a dark cave, covered with trees so tall
That our oaks would seem like bushes next to them,
Two tall old people, naked, sinister and majestic.
They were Eve, with her hair turned white, and her husband,
Adam, pale and pensive, worn out by work,
Carrying the vision of God before him.
Both seated themselves on a rock,
In the midst of mountains with their beetling brows,
And the awesome eternity of the heavens.
Their sad gaze made nature austere;
And there, without a word passing their lips,
With their hands in their laps and their backs to each other,
Bowed down like those who carry great burdens,
Without any sign of life but
Their heads bending further down every hour,
Plunged into a dreary, ominous, dazed state,
Chilled, pale, haggard, bowed
Under the weight of the faceless, limitless infinite,
One gazed at the light dimming, the other at the darkness growing;
And while the constellations rose,
And the first waves gave a long nocturnal kiss
To the first halcyons in the sky,
And, like flowers tumbling out of a vase,
The swarming stars filled the dark sky,

They dreamed, and dreaming, without hearing or seeing,
Deaf to the sounds of the seas whence hurricanes burst forth,
All night, in the darkness, they silently wept;
Both these ancestors of the human race wept,
The father over Abel, the mother over Cain.

Marine-Terrace, September 1855.

(*Les Contemplations*, V)

The Idyll of Plumet Street

The revolutionary sense is a moral sense. The sentiment of rights, developed, develops the sentiment of duty. The law of all is liberty, which ends where the liberty of others begins, according to Robespierre's admirable definition. Since '89, the entire people has been expanding in the sublimated individual; there is no poor man, who, having his rights, has not his ray; the starving man feels within himself the honor of France; the dignity of the citizen is an interior armor; he who is free is scrupulous; he who votes reigns. Hence incorruptibility; hence the abortion of unnoxious lusts; hence the eyes heroically cast down before temptations. The revolutionary purification is such that on a day of deliverance, a 14th of July, or a 10th of August, there is no longer a mob. The first cry of the enlightened and enlarging multitudes is: death to robbers! Progress is an honest man; the ideal and the absolute pick no pockets. By whom in 1848 were the chests escorted which contained the riches of the Tuileries? by the ragpickers of the Faubourg Saint Antoine. The rag mounted guard over the treasure. Virtue made these tatters resplendent. There was there, in those chests, in boxes hardly closed, some even half open, amid a hundred dazzling caskets, that old crown of France all in diamonds, surmounted by the regent's carbuncle of royalty, which was worth thirty millions. Barefooted they guarded that crown.

No more Jacquerie then. I regret it on account of the able. That is the old terror which has had its last effect, and which can never henceforth be employed in politics. The great spring of the red spectre is broken. Everybody knows it now. The scarecrow no longer scares. The birds take liberties with the puppet, the beetles make free with it, the bourgeois laugh at it.

(*Les Misérables*, IV.
Translation taken from *Les Misérables*,
translated by Charles E. Wilbour.
London: John Lane, The Bodley Head Ltd., 1934.
Used by permission.)

THE TWO DUTIES: TO WATCH AND TO HOPE

This being so, is all social danger dissipated? Certainly not. No Jacquerie. Society may be reassured on that account; the blood will rush to its head no more, but let it take thought as to the manner of its breathing. Apoplexy is no longer to be feared, but consumption is there. The consumption of society is called misery.

We die undermined as well as stricken down.

Let us not weary of repeating it, to think first of all of the outcast and sorrowful multitudes, to solace them, to give them air, to enlighten them, to love them, to enlarge their horizon magnificently, to lavish upon them education in all its forms, to offer them the example of labor, never the example of idleness, to diminish the weight of the individual burden by intensifying the idea of the universal object to limit poverty without limiting wealth, to create vast fields of public and popular activity, to have, like Briareus, a hundred hands to stretch out on all sides to the exhausted and the feeble, to employ the collective power in the great duty of opening workshops for all arms, schools for all aptitudes and laboratories for all intelligences, to increase wages, to diminish suffering, to balance the ought and the have, that is to say, to proportion enjoyment to effort and gratification to need, in one word, to evolve from the social structure for the benefit of those who suffer and those who are ignorant, more light and more comfort; this is, let sympathetic souls forget it not, the first of fraternal obligations, this is, let selfish hearts know it, the first of political necessities.

And, we must say, all that is only a beginning. The true statement is this: labor cannot be a law without being a right.

We do not dwell upon it; this is not the place.

If nature is called providence, society should be called foresight.

Intellectual and moral growth is not less indispensable than material amelioration. Knowledge is a viaticum, thought is of primary necessity, truth is nourishment as well as wheat. A reason, by fasting from knowledge and wisdom, becomes puny. Let us lament as over stomachs, over minds which do not eat. If there is anything more poignant than a body agonizing for want of bread, it is a soul which is dying of hunger for light.

All progress is tending towards the solution. Some day we shall be astounded. The human race rising, the lower strata will quite naturally come out from the zone of distress. The abolition of misery will be brought about by a simple elevation of level.

This blessed solution, we should do wrong to distrust.

The past, it is true, is very strong at the present hour. It is reviving. The revivification of a corpse is surprising. Here it is walking and advancing. It seems victorious; this dead man is a conqueror. He comes with his legion, the superstitions, with his sword, despotism, with his banner, ignorance; within a little time he has won ten battles. He advances, he threatens, he laughs, he is at our doors. As for ourselves, we shall not despair. Let us sell the field whereon Hannibal is camped.

We who believe, what can we fear?

There is no backward flow of ideas more than of rivers.

But let those who desire not the future, think of it. In saying no to progress, it is not the future which they condemn, but themselves. They give themselves a melancholy disease; they inoculate themselves with the past. There is but one way of refusing To-morrow, that is to die.

Now, no death, that of the body as late as possible, that of the soul never, is what we desire.

Yes, the enigma shall say its word, the sphinx shall speak, the problem shall be resolved. Yes, the people, rough-hewn by the eighteenth century, shall be completed by the nineteenth. An idiot is he who doubts it! The future birth, the speedy birth of universal well-being, is a divinely fatal phenomenon.

Immense pushings together rule human affairs and lead them all in a given time to the logical condition, that is to say, to equilibrium; that is to say, to equity. A force composite of earth and of Heaven results from humanity and governs it; this force is a worker of miracles; miraculous issues are no more difficult to it than extraordinary changes. Aided by

science which comes from man, and by the event which comes from
Another, it is little dismayed by those contradictions in the posture of
problems, which seem impossibilities to the vulgar. It is no less capable
of making a solution leap forth from the comparison of ideas than a
teaching from the comparison of facts, and we may expect everything
from this mysterious power of progress, which some fine day confronts
the Orient with the Occident in the depths of a sepulchre, and makes
the Imams talk with Bonaparte in the interior of the great pyramid.

In the meantime, no halt, no hesitation, no interruption in the
grand march of minds. Social philosophy is essentially science and
peace. Its aim is, and its result must be, to dissolve angers by the study
of antagonisms. It examines, it scrutinizes, it analyzes; then it recom-
poses. It proceeds by way of reduction, eliminating hatred from all.

That a society may be swamped in a gale which breaks loose over
men has been seen more than once; history is full of shipwrecks of
peoples and of empires; customs, laws, religions, some fine day, the
mysterious hurricane passes by and sweeps them all away. The civilizations of India, Chaldea, Persia, Assyria, Egypt, have disappeared, one
after the other. Why? we know not. What are the causes of these
disasters? we do not know. Could these societies have been saved? was
it their own fault? did they persist in some vital vice which destroyed
them? how much of suicide is there in these terrible deaths of a nation
and of a race? Questions without answer. Darkness covers the condemned civilizations. They were not seaworthy, for they were swallowed up; we have nothing more to say; and it is with a sort of bewil-
derment that we behold, far back in that ocean which is called the past,
behind those colossal billows, the centuries, the foundering of those
huge ships, Babylon, Nineveh, Tarsus, Thebes, Rome, under the terrible blast which comes from all the mouths of darkness. But darkness
there, light here. We are ignorant of the diseases of the ancient civilizations, we know the infirmities of our own. We have everywhere
upon it the rights of light; we contemplate its beauties and we lay bare
its deformities. Where it is unsound we probe; and, once the disease is
determined, the study of the cause leads to the discovery of the remedy.
Our civilization, the work of twenty centuries, is at once their monster
and their prodigy; it is worth saving. It will be saved. To relieve it, is
much already; to enlighten it, is something more. All the labors of
modern social philosophy ought to converge towards this end. The
thinker of to-day has a great duty, to auscultate civilization.

We repeat it, this auscultation is encouraging; and it is by this persis-tence in encouragement that we would finish these few pages, austere interlude of a sorrowful drama. Beneath the mortality of society we feel the imperishability of humanity. Because it was here and there those wounds, craters, and those ringworms, solfataras, because of a volcano which breaks, and which throws out its pus, the globe does not die. The diseases of a people do not kill man.

And nevertheless, he who follows the social clinic shakes his head at times. The strongest, the tenderest, the most logical have their moments of fainting.

Will the future come? It seems that we may almost ask this question when we see such terrible shadow. Sullen face-to-face of the selfish and the miserable. On the part of the selfish, prejudices, the darkness of the education of wealth, appetite increasing through intoxication, a stupefaction of prosperity which deafens, a dread of suffering which, with some, is carried even to aversion for sufferers, an implacable satisfaction, the me so puffed up that it closes the soul; on the part of the miserable, covetousness, envy, hatred of seeing others enjoy, the deep yearnings of the human animal towards the gratifications, hearts full of gloom, sadness, want, fatality, ignorance impure and simple.

Must we continue to lift our eyes towards heaven? is the luminous point which we there discern of those which are quenched? The ideal is terrible to see, thus lost in the depths minute, isolated, imperceptible, shining, but surrounded by all those great black menaces monstrously massed about it; yet in no more danger than a star in the jaws of the clouds.

(*Les Misérables,* IV)
Translation taken from *Les Misérables,*
translated by Charles E. Wilbour.
London: John Lane, The Bodley Head Ltd., 1934.
Used by permission.

How Brother Becomes Father

Nothing is so admirable as a verdure washed by the rain and wiped by the sunbeam; it is warm freshness. The gardens and the meadows, having water at their roots and sunshine in their flowers, become vases of incense, and exhale all their perfumes at once. All these laugh, sing, and proffer themselves. We feel sweet intoxication. Spring is a provisional paradise; sunshine helps to make man patient.

There are people who ask nothing more; living beings who, having the blue sky, say: "it is enough!" dreamers absorbed in marvel, drawing from idolatry of nature an indifference to good and evil, contemplators of the cosmos radiantly diverted from man, who do not understand how anybody can busy himself with the hunger of these, with the thirst of those, with the nakedness of the poor in winter, with the lymphatic curvature of a little backbone, with the pallet, with the garret, with the dungeon, and with the rags of shivering little girls, when he might dream under the trees; peaceful and terrible souls, pitilessly content. A strange thing, the infinite is enough for them. This great need of man, the finite, which admits of embrace, they ignore. The finite which admits of progress, sublime toil, they do not think of. The indefinite, which is born of the combination human and divine, of the infinite and the finite, escapes them. Provided they are face to face with immensity, they smile. Never joy, always ecstasy. To lose themselves is their life. The history of humanity to them is only a fragmentary plan; All is not there, the true All is still beyond; what is the use of busying ourselves with this incident, man? Man suffers, it is possible; but look at Aldebaran rising yonder! The mother has no milk, the new-born dies, I know nothing about that, but look at this marvellous rosette formed by a transverse section of the sapwood of the fir-tree when examined by the microscope! Compare me that with the most beautiful Mechlin lace! These thinkers forget to love. The zodiac has such success with them that it prevents them from seeing the weeping child. God eclipses the soul. There is a family of such minds, at once little and great. Horace belonged to it, Goethe belonged to it, La Fontaine perhaps; magnificent egotists of the infinite, tranquil spectators of grief, who do not see Nero if the weather is fine, from whom the sunshine hides the stake, who would behold the guillotine at work, watching for an effect of light, who hear neither the cry, nor the sob, nor the death-rattle, nor the tocsin, to whom all is well, since there is a month of May, who, so long as there are clouds of purple and gold above their heads, declare themselves content, and who are determined to be happy until the light of the stars and the song of the birds are exhausted.

They are of a dark radiance. They do not suspect that they are to be pitied. Certainly they are. He who does not weep does not see. We should admire and pity them, as we would pity and admire a being at once light and darkness, with no eyes under his brows and a star in the middle of his forehead.

In the indifference of these thinkers, according to some, lies a superior philosophy. So be it; but in this superiority there is some infirmity. One may be immortal and a cripple; Vulcan for instance. One may be more than man and less than man. The immense incomplete exists in nature. Who knows that the sun is not blind?

But then, what! in whom trust? *Solem quis dicere falsum audeat?* Thus certain geniuses themselves, certain Most High mortals, star men, may have been deceived! That which is on high, at the top, at the summit, in the zenith, that which sends over the earth so much light, may see little, may see badly, may see nothing! Is not that disheartening? No. But what is there, then, above the sun? The God.

> (*Les Misérables*, V, I, XVI)
> Comment de frère on devient père.
> Translation taken from *Les Misérables*,
> translated by Charles E. Wilbour.
> London: John Lane, The Bodley Head Ltd., 1934.
> Used by permission.

WILLIAM SHAKESPEARE

What is certain—and this certainty brings about great hope—is that a mighty phenomenon, liberty, is beginning to be seen on earth in man. Using the rigorous language of philosophy and leaving aside obscure possibilities, we can say that it is in man alone that this phenomenon is becoming evident. Of all the entities on earth, only man seems to be free. Whatever is not human, whether it be a thing or an animal, is not free. Assuming this is true, what makes man more privileged than other beings on earth? The capacity to do good or evil . . . the revelation of moral law. For what is the capacity to do good or evil? It is nothing other than liberty and responsibility. . . . Liberty is the soul.

Liberty implies resurrection, for resurrection is responsibility. To carry out its law, that is, for liberty to become responsibility, this phenomenon, which is man himself, must survive after life. Thus, the survival of the soul over the body is definitively proven.

These are sacred mysteries.

Moral law is the thread that we can hold on to in the labyrinth of life.

All the sources of moral law are found in what is called supernaturalism. To deny supernaturalism is not only to be blind to the infinite, but also to reject all virtues. Heroism is a religious affirmation. He who sacrifices himself proves eternity. Nothing finite contains within itself the explanation of sacrifice.

(*William Shakespeare,* reliquat)

OUT OF THE MOUTH OF DARKNESS

Man, as he dreams, descends into the depths of the universe.
I was wandering near the dolmen overlooking Rozel,
At the spot where the headland juts out into a peninsula.
The ghost awaited me; this somber and calm being
Grabbed my hair in his ever-extending hand,
And carried me up to the summit of the dolmen and said:

Know this: everything is aware of its law, its purpose, its path;
Everything in the universe, from heavenly bodies to mites, has ears;
Everything in creation is conscious;
And hearing is a form of seeing,
For things and beings conduct a great dialogue.
Everything speaks: the wind that blows and the halcyon that soars,
The blade of grass, the flower, the seed, the element.
Did you have a different conception of the universe?
Do you think that God, who makes form take on meaning,
Would have given voice to the dark forest,
The storm, the torrent of black silt,
The rock amidst the waves, the animal amidst the mountains,
The fly, the bush, the bramble full of berries,
And that he would have let them murmur endlessly without meaning?
Do you believe that if the water in the rivers and the trees in the woods
Had nothing to say, they would raise their voices?
Do you feel that the sea wind is nothing but a flute player?

Do you think that the ocean, which swells and struggles,
Would be content to open wide its maw night and day
Only to whisper meaningless sounds into the void,
And that it would roar during hurricanes
If its roar was not meaningful?
Do you believe that the grave, covered in grass and darkness,
Is eternally silent? And do you think
That all creation, with its multifarious sounds,
That of lilies and roses,
Of thunder, waves and breezes,
Does not know what it says when it addresses God?
Do you think that creation has only an unrefined tongue?
Do you believe that vast nature stammers?
And that the great Lord's
Only pleasure for eternity
Would be listening to the stuttering of a deaf-mute?
No, the abyss is a priest and the darkness a poet;
No, everything is a voice and everything a fragrance;
Everything says something to someone in the universe;
Thoughts fill the splendid uproar.
God has created no sound without adding meaning to it.
Everything either groans like you or sings like me;
Everything speaks. And now, man, do you know why
Everything speaks? Listen carefully. It is because everything—winds,
    waves, flames,
Trees, reeds and rocks—is alive!

Everything teems with souls.

How can that be? Ah! That is the extraordinary mystery.
Since you are still with me,
Let us pursue our conversation.

God created only the imponderable being.
He made it radiant, beautiful, guileless, adorable,
But imperfect; had he not done so, his creature would have been on a
    level
With him, equal to the creator;
And this perfect being, lost in the infinite,
Would have been confused with God,

And creation, by dint of its perfection,
Would have become one with him and thus would not have existed.
The sacred creation of which the prophets dream
Must, oh wisdom, be imperfect in order to exist.

Thus God created the universe, and the universe created evil.

The created being, adorned by the light of dawn,
In an age which we alone can recall,
Floated in splendor on wings of glory,
Surrounded by song, incense, flame and light;
This being flew around on its golden wings in a dazzling ray of light,
And absorbed all scents one by one;
Everything floated; everything flew.

But the first sin
Was the first burden.
God felt grief.
The burden took on a form, and like the bird-catcher
Who flees with the quivering, struggling bird,
It fell, dragging the lost angel along with it.
The harm was done. And then everything became worse.
And the ether became air, and the air, wind;
The angel became spirit, and the spirit, man.
Evil multiplying the burden, the soul
Was trapped in animals, in trees, and even in more lowly beings
Such as pensive pebbles, those horrible blind creatures;
Vile beings that the angels listed regretfully!
And from this mass, spheres were formed,
And behind these blocks rose the somber darkness.
Evil is matter. Fatal tree, fatal fruit.

(Ce que dit la bouche d'ombre.
1–82)

From one point of view, however, man is unfettered.
The nonman is bound by the yoke, while man is free.
Dreamer, remember this: man represents a balance.
Man is a prison wherein the soul remains free.
Man's soul acts, wisely at times, wrongly at other times;

It rises towards the spiritual level, only to fall back to the animal level;
And, to ensure that nothing impedes the soaring upwards
Of his conscience endowed with wings and absorbed by God alone,
When a soul is born in man who is inclined to good,
God breaks the thread of memory that binds him to his past;
Hence, night has more knowledge than dawn;
The nonman knows itself better than does man.
The nonman symbolizes suffering, man stands for action.
Man is the only one of God's creations
Whose soul, in order to remain free and to improve,
Must forget its former life.
Mystery! On the threshold of knowledge, the mind dreams, dazzled.
Man does not see God, but he can approach him
By following the light of good, which is always shining.
The nonman—trees, rocks, and roaring animals—
Can see God, but remains chained far away from him. And that is its
    ordeal.

Man has love as wings and need as a yoke.
The shadow, which he himself has cast, is on all he sees;
Darkness emerges from his eyes like smoke;
Man, you know nothing; you move forward, growing pale!
At times the dark veil shrouding you, oh passerby,
Flies off and floats away in the wind blowing from another sphere;
Its folds billow out for a moment right up into the light,
And then fall back over you, ghostly being, and everything grows dark
    again.
Your wise men and philosophers have tried to penetrate the darkness;
But what have these sons of Eve seen or done or said?
Nothing. . . .

Man! About you, all creation is a-dreaming
A thousand unknown beings surround your walls.
You move to and fro and fall asleep right before their dim eyes,
And you are unaware of their being alive just as you are.
An entire legion of souls is under your domination;
While it pities you, you trample it underfoot.
Your every move towards the light is carefully watched by the darkness.
What you call thing, object or still life

Knows, thinks, listens and hears. The gates of your being
See your sin approaching and wish to close shut.
Your window recognizes the dawn, and cries: See! Believe! Love!
The curtains around your bed flutter as you dream.
When, oh dreamer, in wicked plans you become involved,
From the heart of the sepulchral hearth, the ashes exclaim:
Behold! I am the remnants of evil.
Alas! Imprudent man betrays, tortures and oppresses.
From the depths of its hell, the nonman sees both ends of crime;
A wolf could give wise counsel to Nero.
Oh man! Blind eagle, inferior to a gnat!
While in your palace or in your cottage,
You do dwell, without even being able to spell the name
Of the first of the constellations, that dark alphabet that gleams
And trembles on the vast page of night,
While you curse and deny God,
While you say: No! to stars and geniuses,
No! to the ideal, No! to virtue, and for no apparent reason,
While you hold yourself above the law,
Imitating thus the anxious or strong disdain
Of those wise men consecrated in ancient busts,
And while you say: What do I know? as, bitter, cold and unbelieving,
You demean your mouth with the hollow laugh of nothingness,
Through the jungle of immense nature,
Scenting eternity with its misshapen snout,
There, in the shadows at your feet, man, your dog sees God.
Ah! I hear you say:—What sorrow! Animals amount to little,
Men to nothing. Oh wretched law! Darkness! Depths!—
Oh dreamer! this wretched law is sublime.
Must everything be repeated to penetrate your puny mind?
Fate, the law of the captive nonman,
Gives way to duty, the fate of man.
Thus the ordeal comes full circle.
From the passive nonman to intelligent man,
Dismal necessity is changed into duty,
And the soul, regaining its pristine beauty,
Moves from the darkness of fate to the light of freedom.
But, I repeat, in order to be transfigured,
And to redeem himself, man must be ignorant.

He must be blinded by every flying particle.
Or else, like a child guided by leading-strings,
Man would head straight for the vision.
Doubt is his strength and his burden.
He sees the rose, and rejects belief; he sees the dawn, and doubts;
There would be no merit in man's discovering his path,
If he, seeing clearly and having complete control over his will,
Had certainty and liberty.
No. He must hesitate in immense nature;
He must live the frightening adventure of making choices;
He must compare vice and its tempting reflection,
And crime and sensual pleasure with the tear-stained eyes of duty;
He must doubt! Yesterday a believer, tomorrow an unbeliever,
He wavers between evil and good; he scans the horizon and plumbs the
    depths;
He wanders back and forth, and trembling, kneeling or standing,
With arms outstretched and a sad heart, he seeks God everywhere.
He probes the infinite until he can touch it;
Then, his winged soul bursts with joy;
The dazzling angel shines bright in transparent man.
Doubt sets him free, and liberty makes him great.
Captivity implies knowing; freedom implies
Hypothesizing, probing, understanding the effect and comparing it to
    the cause,
Believing that it is well-being that it desires, and, in reality, yearning
    for the heavens,
And seeking a pebble but finding a diamond.
This is how the soul slowly takes hold of heaven.

In the nonman, the soul expiates sin; in man, it makes atonement for
    sin.

(Ce que dit la bouche d'ombre.
413–516)

Dream

Yes, far from being a defect, as superficial critics believe, this fabric
of dream inherent in the poet is a supreme gift. It is needful that there

be in the poet a philosopher, and something to boot. He who is lacking in this celestial quality, the dream, is a philosopher only.

This *quid divinum* is revealed by Voltaire in his *Tales*. There alone he is a poet. A striking thing to remark, in his *Tales*. Voltaire dreams, and thinks all the more. He issues out of reality and enters into truth. This draft of imagination, drunk by his reason, transfigures him, and this reason becomes divination. Voltaire in his *Tales* divines and lovingly divines the conclusion, nay more, the final catastrophe of the eighteenth century—a catastrophe which would have shocked him as historian. He invents, he imagines, he permits himself conjecture, he loses his foothold, he takes flight. Behold him in the blue empyrean of hypotheses and theories. Starry thought, up to then, had been chained. It is the apparition of the goddess. *Patuit dea.*

In all the other works of the great Arouet there is the restraint caused by the disquieting influence of the master; the necessity of pleasing power creates a countercurrent to good faith: *Is Trajan satisfied?* This cringing reappears incessantly. The courtier embarrasses the thinker. The valet gives bad advice to the Titan; at Versailles he is a gentleman in ordinary; at Potsdam he has his own keys behind his back. Hence platitude when face to face with fact; while in the sphere of imagination the mind recovers its freedom. Candide is sincere; Micromégas is at his ease. When you can be in Sirius at a stride, you are free. In history Voltaire is hardly a philosopher; in the tale he is almost an apostle.

Poets, behold the mysterious law: Go to excess. Let blockheads translate it by *extravagare.* Go to excess; be extravagant, like Homer, like Ezekiel, like Pindar, like Solomon, like Archilochus, like Horace, like Saint Paul, like Saint John, like Saint Jerome, like Tertullian, like Petrarch, like Alighieri, like Cervantes, like Rabelais, like Shakespeare, like Milton, like Mathurin Régnier, like Agrippa d'Aubigne, like Molière, like Voltaire. Be extravagant with the learned, the just, the wise. *Quos vult AUGERE, Jupiter dementat.*

What pedants style caprice, the imbecile unreason, the ignorant hallucination, what formerly was called sacred madness, what to-day, accordingly as it is one or the other aspect of the dream, is called melancholy or fantasy, that singular state of soul which, persisting in all the poets, has maintained as realities, abstractions, symbols, the lyre, the muse, the tripod, invoked or evoked unceasingly—those strange overtures to unknown inspiration are essential to the profound life of art. Art voluntarily respires the irrespirable. To suppress that is to prevent communication with the infinite. The poet's thought ought to be on a level with extra-human horizons.

Silenus, according to Epicurus, was so pensive a sage that he seemed to be of disordered mind. He became besotted with the infinite. He meditated so deeply upon things that he passed beyond the bounds of life, and one would have said that he was overcome with wine. This wine was the terrible wine of revery.

The complete poet beholds life in a triple vision: Humanity, Nature, the Supernatural. As regards Humanity and Nature, Vision consists in observation; as regards the Supernatural, Vision is intuition.

A precaution is essential here; one must fill oneself with human science. Above all and in spite of all, be a man. Do not fear to surcharge yourself with humanity. Ballast your mind with reality and then throw yourself into the sea.

The sea is inspiration.

• • • •

Every dream is a struggle. The possible does not verge upon the real without a certain mysterious anger. A brain may be devoured by a chimera.

Who has not seen a certain horrible drama unfolded among the tall grass in the springtime. The May-bug, a poor undeveloped larva, has buzzed and fluttered about, met with accidents in dashing itself against walls, trees, men; it has fed upon every branch of green that it could find, it has beat against every glass where it saw the light; it was not life, but a groping, an attempt toward life. One fine evening it falls to the ground; it is eight days old; it is a centenarian. It dragged itself through the air; it drags itself along the ground; it crawls exhausted through the tufts of grass, and the moss; pebbles halt it, a grain of sand impedes it, the tiniest bit of spear-grass is an obstacle to its progress. All of a sudden as it is rounding a blade of grass, a monster descends upon it. It is a beast who has been lying there in ambush, a necrophore, the *jardinière*, a splendid and agile scarabaeus, green purple and flaming gold, a piece of jewelry armed, which runs and has claws. It is a warrior insect, helmed, cuirassed, spurred, caparisoned: the chevalier brigand of the grass.

Nothing is more formidable than to see it issue from the shadow, sudden, unexpected, extraordinary. It hurls itself upon the traveler.

The aged creature has no strength left, its wings are dead, it can not escape. Now something terrible happens. The scarabaeus lays open the insect's belly, into which it plunges its head, then its leathern corselet; it digs and scoops, disappears up to its middle in the wretched creature and eats it alive upon the spot. The victim writhes, struggles, makes despairing efforts, catches at the grass, pulls, tries to fly, and drags along the monster which is eating it.

Such is man in the grip of madness. There are dreamers who are like this poor insect, who have never learned to fly and who can not walk; the dream, dazzling and formidable, hurls itself upon them, empties them, devours them, destroys them.

Revery is a species of digging. To leave the surface, either to mount or to descend is always adventure. To descend, especially, is a grave act. Pindar hovers, Lucretius plunges. Lucretius takes the greater risk. Asphyxia is more formidable than a fall. Hence more disquiet among lyric poets who explore the ego than among lyric poets who take soundings in the skies. The "I" is the dizzy spiral. To explore it excessively strikes terror into the dreamer.

For the rest, all the regions of dreamland should be ventured upon with caution. These encroachments upon the darkness are not without danger. Revery has its dead, madmen. One encounters here and there in these shadows corpses of intelligence, Tasso, Pascal, Swedenborg. These explorers of the human soul are miners exposed to great danger. Sinister things happen at these depths. There occur explosions of firedamp.

The antique Olympus almost made visible this promontory of dreams whose shadow we have shown projected upon the human mind. In Olympus there appears the summit of the dream. The chimeras proper to the thought of man have never become plastic to that extent. The mythological dream is almost palpable, a fact due to the definiteness of its form.

(*Promontorium Somnii.*
Translation taken from *Victor Hugo's*
Intellectual Autobiography, by Lorenzo O'Rourke.
New York and London: Funk & Wagnall Co., 1907.)

What folly to write such words! To expect life after death! What proof do we have of it? What makes us sure of it? The survival of the self is only a mirage. The synonym of faith is gullibility. Immortality is an obsession. And this is grist to the skeptics' mill. I know some good skeptics who formally call themselves atheists, including the late Senator Vieillard, who set some store by the intelligence of Catholics and clericals. It is obvious that clericals do not believe a word they say; they are shrewd; so they are highly thought of. But religious philosophers, pure deists, are by no means hypocrites; they get nothing out of their beliefs; they are obviously fools; so they are ridiculed. The mockery of the skeptics is all-encompassing and contemptuous. They have such magnificent certainty! They possess such knowledge and wisdom! To exist no more is such a fine future! What happiness lies in disappearing, fading away, vanishing, in becoming smoke, ashes, a shadow, in never having existed! What encouragement for existing! It is so nice to hope for Nothing! And these skeptics gather around the believers and scoff. The visionaries of life are jeered at by the visionaries of nothingness. So be it. I, too, have my dream. Leave me free to believe in my nothingness as a n.an and my eternity as a soul. I feel the immense atom within me.

As we have already said, man needs to dream.

For man, dream is a way to escape real life. It is a formidable flight, a dangerous jail break, a scaling of the heights of the impossible, a suspension in abysses on floating ladders, an oft-likely fall. As we have already indicated, this fall is madness.

When man has no dreams of his own, he sets about finding some. Tea, coffee, cigars, pipes, hookahs, perfume-pans and censers are all conducive to dreams.

In this state of somnolence interspersed by flashes of insight, a state that the Turks call kief, life seems to be taking a respite, the soul and the body appear to coexist in a sort of harmonious detachment, with the body almost as much at rest as in the tomb and the soul almost as free as in death. Phantasmagoria both soothes and frightens the dreamer. It is at the same time a delightful and dismal state. Caught up in this semi-intoxicated condition for the last four thousand years, Asia has been tottering, and therefore not progressing. Arabia has hashish and China opium. Today, the West is seeking oblivion in tobacco, that somber sandman of European civilization. Narcotics are the instruments of despotism. Tyrants fade away in dreams; monsters become blurred in visions. How sad it is when man comes to the point of being satisfied with the freedom of idle dreams!

Such consolation is a degradation. It is high time to take measures to avoid it. Be that as it may, man continues to dream.

Did nature not dream its dreams at one time? Was the world not shaped by a dream? Did reverie not figure in the first attempt at creation? Could one not glimpse a dream-like incoherence in the mastodon, the mammoth, the paleonthere, the giant dinothere, the ichtyosaurus, and the pterodactyl? Matter in the state of nightmare was Behemoth; the chaos turned into an animal was Leviathan. It is difficult to deny that these creatures existed, for the remains of these dreams are now in our museums. It seems absurd to imagine ferns five hundred feet tall, and yet coal-pits bear witness to them. What seems impossible today was possible in yesteryears, as anthracites and fossils reveal. To what degree then did the legendary exist? That is an incommensurable problem.

(*Promontorium Somnii*)

THE FUTURE, HOPE

OPENING IN CLOUDY SKIES
Éclaircie

The ocean glitters under the vast cloud.
The waves, worn out by their constant struggle,
Grow drowsy, and, leaving the reefs in peace,
Lap caressingly against the never-ending shore.
It would seem that everywhere, at the same time, life
Does away with evil, grief, winter, darkness, and envy,
And that the dead from their graves call to the living on earth
To love, and that an unknown soul, alive in everything,
Gently brings its lips close to ours.
The being, appeasing its passions in darkness and rapture,
Opening wide its many flanks, breasts, eyes and hearts,
Absorbs from all sides through its deep pores
The sacred sap.
The great peace of the heavens sweeps down like the tide.
The blade of grass flutters in between the cobblestones.

And the soul is alive with passion. The buds seem to have opened.
The infinite seems filled with the quivering of foliage.
It appears to be that magic hour when the earth, awakened,
Hears the sounds of the break of day,
The stirring of wind, work, love,
And man, and the clang of the bolt being drawn,
And the neighing of that white horse, the dawn.
Like a crazy spirit, the sparrow, with a flap of its wings,
Swoops down to tease the colossal wave that smiles;
The air plays with the fly and the foam with the eagle;
The solemn farmer ploughs his furrows and rules
The page on which the poem of corn will be written;
Some fishermen are convivially seated under a vine shoot;
The horizon seems like a dazzling dream in which floats
The scale of the sea, the feather of the cloud,
For the ocean is a hydra and the cloud a bird.
A gleam, a vague ray, shines forth from the cradle
Rocked by a woman on the threshold of a cottage,
And casts a glow upon the fields, the flowers, the water, and becomes
    light
As it touches a grave in the shadow of the church tower.
The light dips down into the depths of the abyss in search of
Darkness, and bestows a kiss on its forehead beneath the dark and wild
    waters.
All is gentle and calm and serene and at peace; God looks on.

Marine-Terrace, July 1855.

(Les Contemplations, VI, X)

WILLIAM SHAKESPEARE

Thought is power.
All power is duty. Should this power enter into repose in our age?
Should duty shut its eyes? and is the moment come for art to disarm?
Less than ever. The human caravan is, thanks to 1789, arrived on a
high plateau; and the horizon being more vast, art has more to do. This

is all. To every widening of horizon corresponds an enlargement of conscience.

(*William Shakespeare*, VI,
Le beau serviteur du vrai, IV.
Translation taken from *William Shakespeare*.
London and New York: The Chesterfield
Society, n. d.)

It is not the Caesar, it is the thinker, who can say when he expires, "Deus fio." So long as he remains a man his flesh interposes between other men and him. The flesh is a cloud upon genius. Death, that immense light, comes and penetrates the man with its aurora. No more flesh, no more matter, no more shade. The unknown which was within him manifests itself and beams forth. In order that a mind may give all its light, it requires death. The dazzling of the human race commences when that which was a genius becomes a soul. A book within which there is something of the ghost is irresistible.

(*William Shakespeare*, Conclusion.
Après la mort, I.
Translation taken from *William Shakespeare*.
London and New York: The Chesterfield
Society, n. d.)

PROGRESS

Progress sometimes rushes headlong, spurred by its dynamic force,
And good, bounding forward, frightens those that it saves.
Move on! Quicken your pace! The horizon is widening.
Go on! Rise! At every stage a larva can be glimpsed;
It is the future appearing in a strange guise;
The future seems like a ghost before it appears as an angel.
Move forth! Whoever wishes to draw closer to it must be ready
For great battles of every kind; man would be deceiving himself
If he thought that God can be reached without effort and hell
Can be done away with without struggle and strife.
The birth of better times involves much pain.
Everything in the heavens is achieved by revolutions.
Progress is nothing but a radiant disaster,

Falling down like a bomb and staying up like a star.
The future approaches like a great gust of wind;
It brutally pushes nations forward;
It causes earthquakes beneath the gallows;
Beneath the mistaken opinion that it silences,
Beneath all that is cowardly, atrocious, vile and petty,
It abruptly digs dark holes in which evil is engulfed.
Go on, struggle, mind of man! It must not be imagined
That good is easily found.
Good is amazing; and the soul is afraid as it brings it into being;
Good has the untamed majesty of a giant
When, foaming, and making a confused clamor,
It emerges like a lion from its den, or like a wave from a lock.
Yes, progress is the water that rises in the night;
It rises; it is a torrent; it is the chastisement
Of the past that it destroys; it approaches; there is no escaping it;
It rises; it is a tide; it rises; it is the deluge!
Dark flood of happiness! Oh terror!
Says man. And genius, that unconquerable trailblazer,
Cries: Oh joy! Move on, mind of man! Move forward!
Accept the vast collusion of plagues!
Go forth! Yes, often, questionable for those who wished it,
Progress, with its blinding light,
Takes on a terrifying, savage appearance
When it crushes the false, the despicable and the horrible.
Its promise is threatening; and for all that is to
Fall, die, end in the dawning day,
False gods, false priests, evil wise men, dishonest judges,
Its laugh is the rictus of the imposing dawn.
Since Adam and Noah, from time to time,
Progress, which relentlessly pursues those it has conquered,
Which wants men to be, to move on, to seek and to shape,
Pushes into the battle its heavenly legions,
Its spangled, ethereal thinkers in the firmament,
All its Olympians clothed in a patch of sky,
Euler, the sidereal, and the magnificent Epicurus;
And like the Chouans in the remote Vendée,
The men of the past, ungainly, troubled and nebulous,

Say when they see them: Let us flee! Here come the recruits!
And those divine men, those heavenly beings,
Bestow their blessings in step with their anger.
Good takes hold of evil and crushes it in its turn.
Accept the invincible blaze of light,
Man! Go and hurl yourself in those open maws
That are called inventions, innovations, discoveries!
The human mind, constantly seeking God, at times sees
The rays turning into a blaze
When, herding before it the common crowd,
It moves from the serpent of darkness to the serpent of light!
No matter! Do not fear progress clamoring
For the good, the true, the just and the innocent!
Do not fear progress devouring the darkness,
Discovering ideals by dint of algebra,
Rising, by means of geometry and poetry, to God!
Do not fear progress, the conqueror of the heavens,
The sphinx that gives life, the archer that aims at the eternal target,
The mountaineer that scales the sublime and the inaccessible!

                                                   (*Dieu*, L'Ange)

Heaven and earth! if evil prevailed, if everything were
But hard labor followed by an infamous protest,
If the past were to return, if man were given
Slimy, puked water to drink,
If darkness could slight the firmament,
If nothing were true, if nothing were sure,
God would have to hide in shame, nature
Would be nothing but a dastardly and dire deception,
The constellations would shine in vain!
That the empyrean shelters a divine villain,
That behind the star-spangled veil of the abyss
There hides a being who premeditates crimes,
That man who sacrifies all—his time, his tears, his blood—
Is the august plaything of the faint-hearted Almighty,
That the future is made up of dark deeds,
That is what I, for my part, refuse to believe.

No, it would not be worthwhile for the wind
To stir up the stormy waves of the living,
For dawn to break through the sea, scattering
Diamond-like drops of dew on vaguely dazzled flowers,
For birds to sing, and for the world to be,
If fate was but a hunter on the watch,
If man's every endeavor gave rise to an illusion,
If darkness was man's daughter and ashes his mother,
If he strove night and day, wishing, bleeding, creating,
Only to reach the dreadful void!
No, I do not accept this bankruptcy,
This ending up with nothing, nothing at journey's end!
No, the Infinite is incapable of that.
What! To shun Charybdis and fall into Scylla!
No, Paris, you great fighter, France, you great star,
By doing your duty, you put God into your debt.
Arise! Fight!

I realize that God seems vague
When seen through the dreadful lattice of fate.
I repeat that this God has often through the ages
Been the cause of much shaking of wise old heads;
I know that the Unknown Being does not respond
To dismal, clumsy calculation or to the scalpel;
So be it. But I have faith. The law is the exalted light.
My conscience is nothing other than God who is my guest.
By tracing a false circle by using false compasses,
I can place him outside the limits of heaven, but never outside myself.
He is my rudder in the waters where I navigate.
If I listen to my heart, I hear a dialogue.
There are two entities within me: him and myself.
He is my only hope and my only fear.
If, perchance, I dream about a sin I would like to commit,
I hear a deep roar within me;
And I ask: Who is it? Is someone speaking to me? Why?
And my soul, trembling, answers: It is God. Be silent.

What! Can I deny progress on earth to which
The vast combined movement of the world adheres?

Certainly not! If it should happen that God deceived me,
And that he filled me with hope as bait
To lure me into the trap, and catch me, a humble entity,
Between the present that is a dream and the future that is a ghost;
If he had no goal other than mockery;
If he, the false vision, deluded me,
A sincere beholder, with some abominable mirage;
If, on the one hand, he gave me a compass, and, on the other, he
    shipwrecked me,
If, through my conscience, he distorted my reasoning;
I, who am only a slight shadow on the horizon,
I, who am nothing, would be his sinister accuser;
I would call upon the vast heavens to bear witness;
I would turn the whole infinite against God;
I believe that the abysses would side wholeheartedly with me.
Against this wrongdoer, I would call the stars as witnesses;
I would lay the blame for our troubles and disasters on him;
I would have the entire ocean to wash my hands of him.
He would make my mistakes as he would have followed my path;
I would be the innocent one and he the guilty one.
This inaccessible, invisible, intangible being,
I would go and see and grab hold of
In the heavens, as one would catch a wolf in the woods;
And in a terrifying, indignant, calm and extraordinary manner,
I would denounce him to his own creation, thunder!
Oh! If evil were the only thing remaining,
If great falsehood were the basis of all,
Everything would be in revolt! Oh! Man would no longer
See the heavens as a temple;
In creation full of a vile secret,
He would no longer see a pillar of glory
But a stake of servitude and poverty.
To this stake would be bound the deceiver
To whom all would cry shame, and at whom would be hurled
Insults from below by our sorrows, our rags, our pallets,
Our hunger, our thirst, our vices and our crimes;
Towards him would be turned our executioners, his victims,
And war and hatred, and eyes bursting with knowledge,

And the bleeding stump of despair;
From the fields, the woods, the mountains, the poisonous flowers,
From the wild and mad chaos of fate,
From all that appears, disappears and reappears,
Would rise a doleful accusation.
The truth would trickle through dreadful cracks;
The comets would appear twisting their tails;
The air would say: He leaves me at the mercy of squalls!
The worm would say to the star: He is envious of you,
And, to humiliate you, he makes both of us glitter!
The reef would say: He is the one who orders me to do harm!
The sea would say: He is my venom. I confess it!
And the universe would be the pillory of God!

Ah! reality is a sublime payment;
And I am the self-assured creditor of the abyss;
My eyes, which are already open, await the great awakening.
No, I do not doubt the abyss of the heavenly bodies!
How can I believe that the darkness is a void when I see the stars
    coming out?
How could the vast, dark sky, the well of dawn,
Be dishonest and make promises it disregards?
It is not possible. The source of the day will be the source of the future.
Nature pledges its word to fate;
Dawn is an eternal promise.
The darkness up above obscures the light.
It is in the darkness that, seeking and dreaming, we believe;
The sky is overcast, dark and mysterious; but it matters not.
Nothing that is just ever knocks on this door in vain.
Complaint is a futile cry, evil an empty word;
I have fulfilled my duty, as I should, and I suffer but am happy,
For all justice is within me, a grain of sand.
When one has done all one can, it is up to God,
And I move forward, knowing full well that nothing will give me the
    lie,
Sure of the integrity of the deep firmament!
And I cry: Hope! to all who love and think;
And I declare that the Unknown Being that

Is free with splendors, flowers, universes, stars, seasons, and winds,
As if he were dipping into ever-open bags,
The Being that constantly lavishes
On mountains piercing the clouds, on waters eroding the sea walls,
The sky, lightening, light and the heavens;
The Being that pours out a torrential flood
Of light, life and love into space,
The Being that does not die or pass on,
The Being that made the world, a book poorly interpreted by priests,
The Being that gives the absolute the form of beauty,
The Being that is real despite doubt and true despite fables,
The eternal, the infinite, God cannot be insolvent!

(*L'Année terrible*, XII)

WHAT HORIZON IS VISIBLE FROM THE TOP OF THE BARRICADE

Enjolras was standing on the paving-stone steps, his elbow upon the muzzle of his carbine. He was thinking; he started, as at the passing of a gust; places where death is have such tripodal effects. There came from his eyes, full of the interior sight, a kind of stifled fire. Suddenly he raised his head, his fair hair waved backwards like that of the angel upon his sombre car of stars, it was the mane of a startled lion flaming with a halo, and Enjolras exclaimed:

"Citizens, do you picture to yourselves the future? The streets of the cities flooded with light, green branches upon the thresholds, the nations sisters, men just, the old men blessing the children, the past loving the present, thinkers in full liberty, believers in full equality, for religion the heavens; God priest direct, human conscience become the altar, no more hatred, the fraternity of the workshop and the school, for reward and for penalty notoriety, to all, labor, for all, law, over all, peace, no more bloodshed, no more war, mothers happy! To subdue matter is the first step; to realize the ideal is the second. Reflect upon what progress has already done. Once the early human races looked with terror upon the hydra which blew upon the waters, the dragon which vomited fire, the griffin, monster of the air, which flew with the wings of an eagle and the claws of a tiger; fearful animals which were above man. Man, however, has laid his snares, the sacred snares of intelligence, and has at last caught the monsters. We have tamed the hydra, and he is called the steamer; we have tamed the dragon, and he is called the locomotive; we are on the point of taming the griffin, we have him already, and he is called the balloon. The day when this promethean work shall be finished, and when man shall have definitely harnessed to his will the triple chimera of the ancients, the hydra, the dragon, and the griffin, he will be the master of the water, the fire, and the air, and he will be to the rest of the animated creation what the ancient gods were formerly to him. Courage, and forward! Citizens, whither are we tending? To science made government, to the force of things, recognized as the only public force, to the natural law having its sanction and its penalty in itself and promulgated by its self-evidence, to a dawn of truth, corresponding with the dawn of the day. We are tending towards the union of the peoples; we are tending towards the unity of man. No more fictions; no more parasites. The real governed by the true, such is the aim. Civilization will hold its courts on the summit of Europe, and later at the centre of the continents, in a grand parliament of intelligence. Something like this has been seen already. The Amphictyons had two sessions a year, one at Delphi, place of the gods, the other at Thermopylae, place of the heroes. Europe will have her Amphictyons; the globe will have its Amphictyons. France bears within her the sublime future. This is the gestation of the nineteenth century. That which was sketched by Greece is worth being finished by France. Listen to me, then, Feuilly, valiant working-man, man of the people, man of the peoples. I venerate thee. Yes, thou seest clearly future ages; yes, thou art right. Thou hadst neither father nor mother, Feuilly; thou has adopted humanity for thy mother, and the right for they father. Thou art going to die here; that is, to triumph. Citizens, whatever may happen to-day, through our defeat as well as through our victory, we are going to effect a revolution. Just as conflagrations light up the whole city, revolutions light up the whole human race. And what revolution shall we effect? I have just said, the revolution of the True. From the political point of view, there is but one single principle: the sovereignty of man over himself. This sovereignty of myself over myself is called Liberty. Where two or several of these sovereignties associate the state begins. But in this association there is no abdication. Each sovereignty gives up a certain portion of itself to form the common right. That portion is the same for all. This identity of concession which each makes to all, is Equality. The common right is nothing more or less than the protection of all radiating upon the right of each. This protection of all over each is called Fraternity. The point of intersection of all these aggregated sovereignties is called Society. This intersection being a junction, this point is a knot. Hence what is called the social tie. Some say social contract; which is the same thing, the word contract being etymologically formed with the idea of tie. Let us understand each other in regard to equality; for, if liberty is the summit, equality is the base. Equality, citizens, is not all vegetation on a level, a society of big spears of grass and little oaks; a neighborhood of jealousies emasculating each other; it is, civilly, all aptitudes having equal opportunity; politically, all votes having equal weight; religiously, all consciences having equal rights. Equality has an organ: gratuitous and obligatory instruction. The right to the alphabet, we must begin by that. The primary school obligatory upon all, the higher school offered to all, such is the law. From the identical school springs equal society. Yes, instruction! Light! Light! all comes from light, and all returns to it. Citizens, the nineteenth century is grand, but the twentieth century will be happy. Then there will be nothing more like old history. Men will no longer have to fear, as now, a conquest, an invasion, a usurpation, a rivalry of nations with the armed hand, an interruption of civilization depending on a marriage of kings, a birth in the hereditary tyrannies, a partition of the peoples by a Congress, a dismemberment by the downfall of a dynasty, a combat of two religions meeting head to head, like two goats of darkness, upon the bridge of the infinite; they will no longer have to fear famine, speculation, prostitution from distress, misery from lack of work, and the scaffold, and the sword, and the battle, and all the brigandages of chance in the forest of events. We might almost say: there will be no events more. Men will be happy. The human race will fulfil its law as the terrestrial globe fulfils its; harmony will be re-established between the soul and the star; the soul will gravitate about the truth like the star about the light. Friends, the hour in which we live, and in which I speak to you, is a gloomy hour, but of such is the terrible price of the future. A revolution is a toll-gate. Oh! the human race shall be delivered, uplifted, and consoled! We affirm it on this barricade. Whence shall arise the shout of love, if it be not from the summit of sacrifice? O my brothers, here is the place of junction between those who think and those who suffer; this barricade is made neither of paving-stones, nor of timbers, nor of iron; it is made of two mounds, a mound of ideas and a mound of sorrows. Misery here encounters the ideal. Here day embraces night, and says: I will die with thee and thou shalt be born again with me. From the pressure of all desolations faith gushes forth. Sufferings bring their agony here, and ideas their immortality. This agony and this immortality are to mingle and compose our death. Brothers, he who dies here dies in the radiance of the future, and we are entering a grave illuminated by the dawn."

Enjolras broke off rather than ceased, his lips moved noiselessly, as if he were continuing to speak to himself, and they looked at him with attention, endeavoring still to hear. There was no applause; but they whispered for a long time. Speech being breath, the rustling of intellects resembles the rustling of leaves.

(*Les Misérables*, V, I, V.
Translation taken from *Les Misérables*,
translated by Charles E. Wilbour.
London: John Lane, The Bodley Head Ltd., 1934.
Used by permission.)

HUGO'S WORKS

1820   Bug-Jargal (2nd version, 1826).
1822   Odes et Poésies diverses.
1823   Han d'Islande.
1824   Nouvelles Odes.
1826   Odes et Ballades.
1827   Cromwell.
1829   Les Orientales.
       Le Dernier Jour d'un Condamné.
       Marion Delorme (performed
       only in 1831).
1830   Hernani.
1831   Notre-Dame de Paris.
       Les Feuilles d'automne.
1832   Le Roi s'amuse.
1833   Lucrèce Borgia.
       Marie Tudor.
1834   Littérature et Philosophie mêlées.
       Claude Gueux.
1835   Angelo Tyran de Padoue.
       Les Chants du Crépuscule.
1836   La Esméralda.
1837   Les Voix intérieures.
1838   Ruy Blas.
1840   Les Rayons et les Ombres.
1842   Le Rhin.
1843   Les Burgraves.
1852   Napoléon le Petit.
1853   Les Châtiments.
1856   Les Contemplations.
1859   La Légende des Siècles.
1862   Les Misérables.
1864   William Shakespeare.
1865   Les Chansons des Rues et des
       Bois.

1866   Les Travailleurs de la Mer.
1869   L'Homme qui rit.
1872   L'Année terrible.
1874   Quatre-Vingt-Treize.
1875   Actes et Paroles, vol. 1, 2.
1876   Actes et Paroles, vol. 3.
1877   La Légende des Siècles, 2.
       L'Art d'être grand-père.
1878   Le Pape.
1879   La Pitié suprême.
1880   Religions et Religion.
1881   Les Quatre Vents de l'Esprit.
1882   Torquemada (written in
       1869).
1883   La Légende des Siècles, 3.
1886   Théâtre en liberté (written for
       the most part in 1869).
       La Fin de Satan (composed in
       1854).
1887   Choses vues, 1.
1888   Toute la Lyre, 1.
1890   Alpes et Pyrénées.
1891   Dieu (composed in large part
       in 1854–55).
1892   France et Belgique.
1893   Toute la Lyre, 2.
1896   Les Années funestes.
1900   Choses vues, 2.
1901   Post-scriptum de ma vie.
1902   Derniére Gerbe.
1942   Océan. Tas de Pierres.

Hugo's works are not presented in their entirety either in the forty-eight-volume edition entitled Oeuvres complètes (Hetzel-Quantin) or in the forty-three-volume "édition nationale" (Emile Testard). The "im-

primerie nationale" edition (Ollendorff, Albin Michel), although far
better, is not complete either. The best editions of Hugo's complete
works are those published by Pauvert (4 vols.) and by Jean Massin,
Club français du Livre (18 vols.). The latter is especially good in that it
contains valuable criticism by various authors.

BIBLIOGRAPHY

Albouy, Pierre. *La Création mythologique chez Victor Hugo.* Paris: Corti, 1963.

———. "La préface philosophique des *Misérables.*" *Bulletin de la Faculté des Lettres de Strasbourg,* no. 5 (February 1962), pp. 315–28.

Barrère, Jean-Bertrand. *La Fantaisie de V. Hugo.* 3 vols. Paris: Corti, 1949, 1950, and 1960.

———. *Hugo. Les Écrivains devant Dieu.* Paris: Desclée de Brouwer, 1965.

———. *Hugo, l'homme et l'oeuvre.* Paris: Hatier (Connaissance des Lettres), 1952.

Baudoin, Charles. *Psychanalyse de V. Hugo.* Geneva: Editions du Mont-Blanc, 1943.

Berret, Paul. *La Philosophie de V. Hugo (1854–1859) et deux mythes de La Légende des Siècles* (Le Satyre, et Pleine Mer, Plein Ciel). Paris: H. Paulin, 1910.

———. "Le Satyre et le panthéisme de V. Hugo." *Revue d'Histoire littéraire de la France,* July–September 1912, pp. 376–81.

———. "V. Hugo et la vie future." *Revue des Deux Mondes,* May 15, 1935, pp. 345–57.

Brombert, Victor. "V. Hugo, la prison et l'espace." *Revue des Sciences humaines,* no. 117 (January–March 1965), pp. 59–80.

Buchanan, Donald. *Les Sentiments religieux de V. Hugo, de 1825 à 1848.* Besançon: Imprimerie de l'Est, 1939.

Coulmas, Danae. "Das Apokalyptische im lyrischen Werk V. Hugos." Hamburg, Romanistiche dissertation, 1966.

Dédeyan, Charles. *V. Hugo et l'Allemagne.* 2 vols. Paris: Minard, Lettres modernes, 1964–65.

Emery, Léon. *Vision et pensée chez Hugo.* Lyon: Audin, n. d.

Gaudon, Jean. *Ce que disent les tables parlantes. Hugo à Jersey.* Paris: Pauvert, 1963.

———. *Le Temps de la contemplation.* Paris: Flammarion, 1969.

Grant, Elliott M. *The Career of V. Hugo.* Cambridge: Harvard University Press, 1945.

———. *The Perilous Quest. Image, Myth and Prophecy in the Narratives of Hugo.* Durham, N. C.: Duke University Press, 1968.

Grillet, Claudius. *La Bible dans V. Hugo*. Paris: Hachette, 1910.

———. *V. Hugo Spirite*. Lyon: Vitte, 1929.

Guille, Frances. *Adèle Hugo. Le Journal de l'Exil*. Vol. I. Paris: Minard Lettres modernes, 1968.

Guillemin, Henri. *Hugo par lui-même*. Paris: Seuil, 1951.

———. "Hugo et le rêve." *Mercure de France* 312 (May 1951), pp. 5–32.

———. *Post-scriptum de ma vie*. A Critical Edition. Neuchâtel: Ides & Calendes, 1961.

Heugel, Jacques. *Essai sur la philosophie de V. Hugo au point de vue gnostique*. Paris: C. Lévy, 1922.

Hunt, Herbert J. *The Epic in Nineteenth Century France*. Oxford: Blackwell, 1941.

Journet, René, and Guy Robert. *Le Mythe du peuple dans les Misérables*. Paris: Éditions sociales, 1965.

———. *Promontorium Somnii*. A Critical Edition. Besançon: *Annales littéraires*, vol. 42, and Belles-Lettres, 1961; and *Dieu*. A Critical Edition. 2 vols. Paris: Nizet, 1960.

Lecoeur, Charles. *La Philosophie religieuse de V. Hugo*. Paris: Bordas, 1951.

Le Dantec, Yves-G. "Hugo poète lyrique." *Revue des Deux Mondes*, June 1, 1935, pp. 658–70.

Levaillant, Maurice. *L'Inspiration mystique de V. Hugo (1843–56)*. Paris: Corti, 1954.

Mabilleau, Léopold. *V. Hugo*. Paris: Hachette, 1893.

Milner, Max. *Le Diable dans la littérature française de Cazotte à Baudelaire*. Vol. II. Paris: Corti, 1960 (Ch. XXVI, pp. 358–422, on *La Fin de Satan*).

Poulet, Georges. "L'espace et le temps chez V. Hugo." *Esprit*, October 1950, pp. 478–505.

Py, Albert. *Les Mythes grecs dans la poésie de V. Hugo*. Geneva: Droz, 1963.

Renouvier, Charles. *V. Hugo le philosophe*. Paris: A. Colin, 1900.

Riffaterre, Michel. "La poésie métaphysique de V. Hugo." *The Romanic Review* 41, no. 4 (December 1960), pp. 268–76.

Rigal, Eugène. *Hugo, poète épique*. Paris: Société française d'Imprimerie et de Librairie, 1900.

———. "La signification du Satyre et la philosophie de V. Hugo, de

1854 à 1859." *Revue d'Histoire littéraire de la France,* January–March 1912, pp. 85–94.

Saurat, Denis. *La Religion de V. Hugo.* Paris: Hachette, 1929 (partially reproduced in *V. Hugo et les dieux du peuple.* Paris: La Colombe, 1948).

Savey-Casard, P. *Le Crime et la peine dans l'oeuvre de V. Hugo.* Paris: Presses Universitaires de France, 1956.

Schwab, Raymond. *La Renaissance orientale.* Paris: Payot, 1950 (Book V, Ch. II: "V. Hugo troublé par l'Inde").

Simon, Gustave. *Les Tables tournantes de Jersey.* Paris: Conrad, 1923.

Stapfer, Paul. *Hugo et la grande poésie satirique en France.* Paris: Ollendorff, 1901.

—————. *V. Hugo à Guernesey.* Paris: Société française d'Imprimerie et de Librairie, 1905.

Thomas, John H. *Hugo et la littérature anglaise.* Paris: Droz, 1934.

Uzanne, Octave. *Les Propos de table de V. Hugo en exil.* Paris: Quantin, 1892.

Venzac, Géraud. *Les Origines religieuses de V. Hugo.* Paris: Bloud & Gay, 1955.

Vial, André. "Un beau mythe de *La Légende des Siècles:* le Satyre." *Revue des Sciences humaines,* no. 87 (July–September 1957), pp. 229–317.

Viatte, Auguste. *Hugo et les illuminés de son temps.* Montréal: L'Arbre, 1942.

Villiers, Charles. *L'Univers métaphysique de V. Hugo.* Paris: Vrin, 1970.

Zumthor, Paul. *V. Hugo poète de Satan.* Paris: Laffont, 1946.

INDEX